DOG TRAINING

BY JASON SMITH

CREATIVE
PUBLISHING
international

CHANHASSEN, MINNESOTA

www.creativepub.com

JASON SMITH is the editor of *Just Labs* magazine and the managing editor of *The Retriever Journal* and *The Pointing Dog Journal*. He has written 5 books and more than 100 articles on training hunting dogs. He holds degrees in wildlife sciences and management. Jason lives in Michigan with his wife, son and two dogs—an English setter and a Labrador retriever.

DEDICATION

For Allie and Josie, and all the canine pals I've shared a duck blind, grouse covert, pheasant field or a Sunday afternoon snooze with. The miles are always shorter when following a four-legged friend.

ACKNOWLEDGMENTS

Dog training is an ever-evolving process, and new equipment, theories, drills,and procedures seem to sprout up every year. And in almost every case, they move the art of dog training to where it should be—that of being a mutual communication between you and your dog and not an imposition of wills.

And it is today's professional trainers who are conveying this communication who deserve all of the credit. Yes, bloodlines of the different breeds have improved, and dogs are being produced that are healthier, and some would say smarter, than their predecessors. But getting into the canine brain and speaking their language in order to get these dogs to do some pretty amazing things is one of the outdoor world's most impressive accomplishments.

Many thanks to all of the trainers and veterinarians who contributed valuable advice and pointers for this work: Dr. Jill Hyland Ayres, Dr. Rose Davidson, John and Amy Dahl, Butch Goodwin, Evan Graham, Charlie Jurney, James Keldsen, Dr. Kyle Kerstetter, Mike Lardy, Rick Smith, and Sharon Potter. Your accomplishments with dogs could fill volumes, and I thank you for taking the time out of your schedules to share your knowledge.

I'd also like to thank my family—my wife Vickie, and my son Pete—for putting up with me sitting in front of a computer while I finished this book. And thanks to Dad for not only doing a good edit on the first draft but also for showing me just how much more fun a hunt is when you're accompanied by a dog.

And thanks to Barbara Harold of CPi for all of her help in guiding this project through the production process. I truly had a wonderful time working with you.

Jason Smith
Traverse City, MI
2003

President/CEO: Michael Eleftheriou

Vice President/Publisher: Linda Ball

Vice President/Retail Sales & Marketing: Kevin Haas

Executive Editor, Outdoor Group: Barbara Harold

Creative Director: Brad Springer

Project Manager: Tracy Stanley

Photo Editor: Angela Hartwell

Director, Production Services: Kim Gerber

Production Manager: Helga Thielen

Production Staff: Laura Hokkanen, Stephanie Barakos

Printed on American paper by: R. R. Donnelley

10 9 8 7 6 5 4 3 2 1

DOG TRAINING
by Jason Smith

Cover Photo: Dale C. Spartas, inset photo: Denver Bryan

Contributing Photographers: Denver Bryan, Alan & Sandy Carey, Daniel Dempster/Dembinsky Photo Assoc., Lon E. Lauber, Bill Marchel, Greg Meader, Sharon Potter, Mark Raycroft, John Schafer, Dusan Smetana, Dale C. Spartas, Ron Spomer

Contributing Illustrator: Chris Smith

Library of Congress Cataloging-in-Publication Data

Smith, Jason A.
 Dog training / by Jason Smith.
  p. cm. -- (The Complete hunter)
 Includes index.
 ISBN 1-58923-115-5
  1. Dogs--Training. 2. Hunting dogs--Training. I. Title.
 II. Complete hunter (Creative Publishing International)

SF431.S614 2003
636.75--dc21
                                                      2003048597

DOG TRAINING

CONTENTS

Introduction

Dogs, like kids, can bring out all sorts of emotions in us as we train them for a specific task and raise them in our household as part of the family. From frustration to joy, disappointment to amazement, training a dog–particularly if it's your first one–can be a roller coaster. You'll go through times when it seems as though nothing is getting through and all hope is lost; then, seemingly overnight, the dog will perform as if he understood you perfectly the entire time–he just finally decided to listen. Always keep in mind that no matter how poorly the dog may be reacting to a lesson, he'll also have a lot of "light-switch moments," when he'll suddenly be listening and the light will magically turn on.

While this book is meant for everyone who decides to buy and train a pointing dog or retriever for hunting and for the family, it is geared toward the hunting dog owner, not the competitive dog owner. A competitive dog will need more specialized training than that described here, most likely one-on-one from a professional. This book is intended for the person who wants to train his or her own dog to hunt effectively and efficiently, keeping in mind that the best training method is that which will produce the qualities you desire in your dog.

People require different things of their dogs. This book will cover all of the basic and some of the advanced skills that every hunting retriever or pointing dog should know in order to be effective, efficient and a joy to hunt with. You may find over the course of your dog's life that he possesses skills he never uses except in training situations, or that he's deficient in skills necessary to make the hunt more complete. In the latter situation, you'll find that it's possible to teach an old dog new tricks. Your observations about your dog will become even more important when you take on that next young pup to train–you'll be more certain of the abilities you want your new dog to master.

Most importantly–and you should keep this fundamental fact in mind throughout the course of your training–the dog is a member of the family. This book will also help you welcome that new member into the household, where he'll spend most of his life– as a couch potato, or swimming with the kids, or going on an evening walk or sacking out with you as you watch the hockey game on ESPN. Allie, my 5-year-old English setter, spends more hours sprawled on our bed than she does pointing ruffed grouse or woodcock; and Josie, my 3-year-old Labrador retriever, follows me more from room to room of the house than to the duck blind.

But no matter how much time your dogs spend as well-adjusted (or maladjusted, depending on who you talk to) family members, they can sense the turn in the air when hunting season rolls around. And then those pieces of their genetic code, the pieces that are still wolf, begin to stir from their long spring and summer slumber and once again yearn to run free. I'll take a shotgun out of the closet in springtime to shoot some targets, and both dogs roll an eye toward me as though to say *Don't let the door hit you on the way out.* Yet if I even *think* about taking the shotgun out in the height of duck or grouse season, they're waiting at the door for me, wondering what's taking so long.

CHAPTER ONE

The Evolution of a Dog Trainer

To be a good dog trainer, you need to be able to "read" your dog—recognize what he's doing wrong or when he's about to do something wrong, and understand when to administer praise or a correction. But it also helps to be able to understand a little canine communication and to communicate in a similar language—that is, to convey what you want in a language the dog understands.

We'll cover those topics later in the book. This chapter, however, is about you, the trainer. It's about the frame of mind you need to be in to effectively and efficiently train your dog to be a cherished member of the house and a valued partner in the field. Consider this chapter a little "trainer training" before you begin dog training.

Like most things in life, successful training depends almost entirely upon *attitude*. Begin this enterprise with the right attitude, and you stand to take only positive steps forward; lose that positive attitude, and the experience will be "one step forward, two steps back." Both the trainer and the dog will be the worse for it.

So let's get one fact out in the open right from the beginning: *Consistency, positive reinforcement* and *patience* will always win out in the end. There will most assuredly be times for discipline, too, to curtail disruptive or destructive behavior; however, you should always first ask yourself if the dog actually knows what is being asked of him before you administer a correction. More often than not, the faults of the dog are the faults of the trainer.

The Stages of a Trainer

Training a dog is similar to riding a roller coaster—lots of ups and downs. You'll find that some days your dog looks like a world beater, and some days you'll wonder if he even knows his name. With that said, my firsthand experience with countless dogs and trainers has proved that most trainers do go through a general progression. You'll proceed through these stages more quickly with each dog you train, but the sooner you understand them, the faster you'll get through them with your first dog.

Stage One. We all get a puppy with dreams of owning a champion or, at the very least, the dog of a lifetime. This feeling is more intense if we're paying a good amount of money for the dog or if the dog comes from champion bloodlines. The raw material is there; it's in the dog's genes to be a champion. This training stuff can't be too hard, can it? We picture posing with our six-month-old at his induction ceremony into the Bird Dog Hall of Fame.

The reality is that it's not going to happen. In fact, this overconfidence is one of the worst frames of mind to have when approaching a new puppy. We should put those dreams of greatness out of our head as soon as we see those big, dark brown puppy-dog eyes staring up at us. This brand-new dog with a brand-new family doesn't need that kind of pressure. If you go the competitive route, a championship dog is the obvious goal; but as I said earlier, this book isn't for competitors.

A proper retrieve by this male golden retriever required training him with both basic and advanced skills.

Don't put too much pressure on the youngster, and be quick with praise when the pup does what you want.

Stage Two. After we've trained that soon-to-be champion for a while, we hit a lot of walls; but the dog still shows enough promise to keep the fires of that "great dog" dream burning in our mind. The Hall of Fame goal is replaced by the desire to have the best dog of all our hunting pals—or at least a dog that will outperform any other dog he hunts with on any given day.

This goal may be a little bit more realistic, but it's still too much pressure and too much to expect, especially if this is our first dog. Hunting dogs are the equivalent of professional athletes. There will be days when they won't be able to hit the curve-ball or make the free throw—just like there are days when we couldn't hit a duck if it were the size of a jumbo jet.

Stage Three. At this point, we go into mainte-nance mode with our training. We continue to stumble through it, and we still push to try new things. Mostly, we cram new lessons into our dog right up to the opening day of hunting season, hoping that if we throw a bunch of things at him, something will stick.

This is the time when we experience something I call a "defining moment," and it's not good. One day we put too much pressure on our dog or lose our temper, and we lash out—in other words, we blow our top. Our dog reacts negatively to the point where we feel terrible. We end up giving the pooch an extra helping of food at dinnertime or letting him sneak up on the couch for the evening news—something that makes us feel like we've made it up to the dog. Our dog forgave us about 2.3 seconds after we spouted off; that's just the nature of the unconditional love that dogs are masters of. But human nature includes the emo-tion of guilt, and no guilt is more powerful than that we put on ourselves.

For me, the defining moment with Allie came when she ate a box of rat poison. As I raced her to the vet clinic to have her stomach pumped, all I could think about—other than the prospect of my dog dying—were the times I lost my temper about things she wasn't doing perfectly. The thought of losing her drove the point home: I wanted new things, fun things, to remember.

Stage Four. After this defining moment, we make a firm commitment to have fun, take everything in stride and be patient. We promise ourselves to let the dog have fun being a dog and doing what he was bred for—and we promise that we'll explain things more clearly next time.

With this new training philosophy, our dog responds better. A little way down the road, he'll make an amazing retrieve on a crippled duck after taking our hand signals. Or he'll pin down a covey of quail and stand rock steady as the birds flush and we shoot. These amazing results of our bumbling training methods—more defining moments, but positive ones—firm up that commitment to be patient and have fun.

Several years later, a new pup comes into the household, and we start back at Stage One. But the good news is that we'll move through the stages faster, and the defining moment with this pup will not be as bad as the first one. The commitment is renewed, and the next time, it's made *before* we get a new pup.

Amateurs and Pros

The point of this entire chapter is that if this is your first pup, I urge you to not go through two or three or ten dogs before you decide on a patient, teaching-oriented training technique. As I said earlier, there will be times for discipline, and you'll need to administer a good swat on the behind every so often. But the bottom line is that the quicker you understand the importance of *having fun* with your dog—both while training and hunting—the better off you and your dog will be.

That understanding is the primary difference between amateur and professional trainers. The level of patience a dog trainer has determines his or her reactions to problems when they arise, and it is in these reactions that the wheat is separated from the chaff. The professional trainer sees a dog's misunderstanding or inability to grasp a concept as an indication of the need for more repetition, a refined drill or a confidence boost in the form of going back to basics. The pro's reaction? Patient repetition, accommodating the dog while getting him to unwittingly comply or perform the

task, and praise at just the right instant. Hey—it's why they get the big bucks.

The amateur, on the other hand, sees the bewildered dog that can't seem to get it right as a personal affront—a product of poor bloodlines or the rebelliousness of youth. Our amateur reaction? Too often it's anger and frustration. But what we actually have is a confused dog that didn't comply simply because he didn't know what we were asking. Now, a pro may be able to respond patiently because he or she has the time and equipment to train dogs all day long, while we amateurs are usually trying to squeeze in the same lessons in the 10 minutes we have after work before it gets dark. It's easy to fly off the handle when we see that time's slipping away to hunting season and our one and only dog still doesn't "get it."

But when it comes down to it, a dog's noncompliance is pretty much the same for both kinds of trainer. So are the first few moments after the incorrect behavior, when both pro and amateur

Consistency, positive reinforcement and patience will always win out in the end.

A new puppy will show you just how much patience you have.

have to react. But where the pro simply confronts the *misunderstanding*, the amateur confronts the dog *and* his own adverse reaction to the problem. Ever throw gasoline on a fire?

One of the big culprits of an amateur's impatience are those silly timetables that say our dog should be doing such-and-such by X months old. Don't listen to them. Many breeds mature and learn at different rates, and every dog within a breed is different. A valuable skill we need to possess as a trainer is the ability to recognize when a dog is or isn't ready for the next step. (There is only one instance when I recommend a training step at a particular age. That's the process of force-fetching, which should be done only *after* the dog has his adult teeth—a purely physical requirement.) So don't listen when your buddies brag about their dogs' tremendous exploits at young ages. Proceed with your own dog according to your dog's abilities.

The Bottom Line

In the end, we need to realize just what we're talking about when we decide to get a hunting/family dog. We're talking about a family companion for twelve months out of the year, a dog we load into the truck to sit in a boat or blind or run the woods or fields for three of those months—usually for only a few hours each day, and most assuredly not every day.

By no means am I suggesting that you not take your dog's training or socialization seriously. It is an extremely important proposition you've entered into, and you owe it to your dog to train him well, both for his safety and so that he knows his place in the family structure. But your hunting dog is not just a tool to get a job done. He is a valued hunting companion—sometimes your only hunting companion—and your training methods should reflect the goal of having a reliable hunting partner with whom you can have a great time.

Once a dog is ready for the field, you'll find it fun to keep track of his performance the same way you keep track of your own. I keep a journal that details the experiences and feelings of the hunt— where we went, who was along, what the weather was like and how many birds I shot, as well as how many points Allie had, or how many retrieves Josie had or how many birds she flushed.

My photo albums of each dog still have many blank pages I intend to fill, and it will be fun to do final tallies at the end of their careers. But it will be not just those points and retrieves, but also the great times sacking out on the couch with them or roughhousing in the living room, that will stay with me when I'm playing with my seventh or eighth or twentieth puppy.

Attitude, consistency, keeping it fun, being firm when necessary, praise and patience—these are the ingredients to making your dog-training experience and the making of a hunting and family companion, as enjoyable as possible.

Once a dog is ready for the field, you'll find it fun to keep track of his performance the same way you keep track of your own.

CHAPTER TWO

Selecting Your New Pup

Though you may have a particular favorite breed of dog that you've always wanted, before selecting your future hunting dog you need to take a close look at the kind of hunting you do the most. Your hunting buddy may have a terrific Labrador retriever that gets a workout every day of the duck season. Maybe you've fallen in love with the dog, and therefore the breed, the few times you've tagged along. But if you duck hunt only two or three times per year and instead hunt bobwhite quail as often as possible, a Lab may not be the best choice.

All things being equal, pointing dogs are upland specialists and retrievers are waterfowl specialists. A few breeds known as continental breeds are considered "versatile" dogs, able to hunt both upland game birds and waterfowl with exceptional ability. These breeds, however, may lack some of the finer points that the breeds developed specifically for upland birds or waterfowl possess. The flushing dogs, primarily the spaniels (of which this book covers only the popular English springer spaniel), are also excellent versatile dogs. The springer is the most popular and well known of the spaniel breeds, and is excellent on waterfowl; most other spaniels are smaller in number and better suited to the uplands.

Are you a dedicated ruffed grouse and woodcock hunter? Do you hunt the eastern shore for Canada geese and sea ducks? Are you the biggest ring-necked pheasant diehard in the country? Or do you like to hunt a smattering of game–doves, sharp-tailed grouse and prairie chickens early in the season; then woodcocks and ruffed grouse; a few trips for pheasants scattered through the duck and goose season; and a shooting-preserve hunt for quail, pheasants and chukars in late winter? Keep in mind that if you can deal with hunting behind a flushing dog in the uplands (which is easier in the open country than in the mountains or woods), it is easier for a retriever to also be a good upland dog than it is for a pointing dog to be a good waterfowl dog.

With all of these breeds, you should do more research, primarily with the American Kennel Club (AKC) and the national breed clubs of each, to see which dog you think is best for your situation. And you should always bear in mind that most of the stereotypes about certain breeds are just that– there are always exceptions. The qualities of your dog depend mostly on the breeder, the dog's parents and the atmosphere in which you raise and train the dog. Some of the toughest, meanest dogs can come from breeds that are supposed to be teddy bears; and some of the best upland hunting dogs may come from lines that were destined for duck blinds. Dogs are individuals, and as someone once told me, "Each dog should be approached differently, as a painter approaches a blank canvas." In other words, you get out of your dog exactly what you put into him.

All of the dogs described below should make good members of the family, provided that you raise and train them as such and that the breeder has proved to have even-tempered dogs that are pleasant around all sorts of people and environments.

Which one is it going to be?

The Pointing Breeds

The four most popular breeds of pointing dogs are the English setter, pointer, Brittany and German shorthaired pointer (which is considered a Continental breed and is covered in that group). These four breeds have found fans among all the upland gamebird pursuits—bobwhite quail, desert quail, prairie grouse (sharp-tailed grouse, prairie chickens and sage grouse), pheasant, ruffed grouse, woodcocks, mountain grouse (blue and spruce grouse), Hungarian partridge and ptarmigan.

If it's a pointer you want, look for a breeder who hunts his or her dogs on the same kind of game you're interested in. But above all else, an ethical breeder with good bird dogs will produce dogs that can hunt all of the above game—even in the same year. Suppose you're a fanatical ruffed grouse and woodcock hunter with a choice between a questionable English setter breeder in your home state who has "great grouse dogs" and a reputable breeder of setters in Arizona that tackle desert

quail all year. My advice? Go with the reputable breeder ten times out of ten.

English Setter. This dog has a long, feathery coat and tail that will require extra care. English setters range in size from little 35-pound ghosts to lumbering 80-pound giants. They are white with black (properly called "blue") spots, white with light brown (properly called "orange") spots, or "tricolor"–white with both blue and orange spots. It is impossible to find two English setters that look alike. Though they have a reputation for being somewhat aloof, they make excellent family dogs; their upland skills have been proven on every species of game bird. Stereotypically, the English setter is most popular as a ruffed grouse and woodcock dog.

Pointer. This short-haired dog has a reputation as a far and fast hunter, and almost all of the pointing-dog field-trial national champions dating back a half-century have been pointers. They are very muscular, even though their bones appear just

English setters make excellent family dogs and their upland skills have been proven on every species of gamebird.

below the surface. Pointers are sometimes incorrectly referred to as English pointers; the "English" was dropped some time ago. They're white with black splotches, white with light brown (properly called "lemon") spots or white with chocolate brown (properly called "liver") splotches. Pointers are the dog of choice for almost all quail hunters, as well as hunters in warm environments.

Brittany. The Brittany originated in France as a "poacher's dog" in the late Middle Ages, used to retrieve game illegally taken by peasants on a lord's land. That retrieving desire still exists today in the breed and is a factor that sways many people to consider the Brit. Brittanys are sometimes incorrectly referred to as Brittany spaniels; the "spaniel" was dropped recently. They're white with large rust-colored markings, and their tail is docked (cut short hours after birth). Most Brittanys are more compact than setters or pointers, though they have remarkable speed for their size. They have been used on all upland gamebirds, and have found an especially ardent following among pheasant hunters.

Other Pointing Breeds. A few other pointing breeds have smaller, dedicated followings. One, the Gordon setter, is a black and tan relative of the English or Irish setter. The hunting Irish setter, also known as the red setter, is usually smaller than the big, feathery Irish setters, which are primarily pets and show dogs. The French Brittany is a little smaller than a Brittany; its markings are white with broad dark blue, orange or tricolor splotches. There are several other breeds with smaller numbers, but they are really beyond the scope of this book.

These other breeds may be harder to find and can command higher prices because of their scarcity, but their gene pools may be more pure and better controlled because breeding has been kept under close supervision. For Irish setters, pay close attention to make sure that you are buying from a field line and not from show or pet stock; the hunting Irish setter could almost be considered a separate, much smaller breed.

The pointer is the dog of choice in warm climates and is a hard runner.

A strong desire to retrieve, a good nose and a warm personality has made the Brittany a popular pointing dog.

The Retrievers

Two of these breeds are the two most popular dogs in the country year after year. The Labrador retriever and the golden retriever have found an unbelievably large following–among hunters; in the service community, where they act in search-and-rescue, bomb- and drug-sniffing, seeing-eye, therapy, and handicap assistance roles; and in the general pet-owning community at large. If you are looking for either of these breeds, you must be extremely careful of puppy mills, which crank out puppies for money only, with no regard to the health or betterment of the breed. You'll have to research the breeders carefully to make sure you are buying from proven hunting lines.

These born-and-bred waterfowl dogs have the makeup for hunting in demanding conditions–a tough water-repellent coat, intensity to get the job done and dedication to tackle any challenge. From Canada goose fields to coastal sea duck blinds, and from prairie potholes to backwoods marshes–if you see a waterfowl hunter, you usually see one of the following dogs in the blind:

Labrador Retriever. With over 150,000 dogs registered every year with the AKC, the Lab is the most popular dog in the country. Labs are black, yellow (shades from almost white to fox red) or chocolate (with some almost a silvery color). Their extreme popularity, especially with "backyard" breeders, will force you to carefully seek out a breeder of hunting Labs. They are probably the best all-around dog you can have in terms of hunting desire, drive, ability, trainability and family companionship. Should you not mind doing your upland hunting–especially pheasants–behind a flushing dog, and if you love to duck hunt, a Lab is probably your best choice.

Golden Retriever. Finding a hunting or field trial line of golden retrievers may be more difficult than with a lab, but it's still very possible. These dogs may be a bit on the "soft" side compared to a Lab, and much more sensitive than a Chesapeake, but they are excellent family dogs.

America's most popular dog–the Labrador retriever.

Their longer coats will require vigilant grooming on your part, but a golden retriever is one of the most handsome—and intelligent—of all the sporting dogs.

Chesapeake Bay Retriever. The rust-colored or dead-grass-colored Chesapeake is almost purely a waterfowl specialist. Indeed, it may be the best duck- and goose-hunting dog in the world in terms of sheer drive and toughness in personality as well as ruggedness in the elements. That toughness can lead to some training problems and has contributed to a stereotype that Chesapeakes are a hard-nosed, even mean, dog. While this may have been the case in the early 1900s during the market-hunting days, modern breeding of Chesapeakes has greatly curtailed their aggressive nature. These days the stereotype is usually perpetuated only by rumors and old wives' tales. Chesapeakes can still be strong-willed, and they most definitely have a mind of their own. So they may not be a wise choice if you're in the market for your first dog. But they are also exceptionally loyal and do not know the meaning of the word "quit."

English Springer Spaniel. This short, feathery flushing dog has a wonderful reputation as a pheasant specialist—it gives relentless pursuit until the bird takes flight, it has great tracking ability, and it's a dependable retriever. The springer's dense coat is white with chocolate-brown or liver splotches; it shows up very well in the uplands. Like that of many other sporting dogs, the tail is docked. Springers have wonderful dispositions around the house, though they may tend to be a bit hyperactive. With some extra training, they can make great waterfowl dogs, but as they lack the water-shedding quality of the retrieving breeds, they may not be able to hunt very late into the season.

Other Retrievers. Several other retriever breeds have smaller followings. Curly-coated retrievers look almost like a poodle with a long tail. Flat-coated retrievers resemble a black golden retriever. The Nova Scotia duck tolling retriever is a golden, longhaired dog that brings in ducks by running or swimming along the shore, an old practice called "tolling." American and Irish water spaniels are smaller dogs ideal for hunting from boats.

(top) You may need to work to find a good line of hunting golden retrievers, but they are exceptionaly intelligent dogs.

(lower right) Springer spaniels are very popular pheasant dogs and have a wonderful disposition around the home.

(lower left) The true waterfowl specialist—the Chesapeake Bay retriever—doesn't know the meaning of the word "quit."

The Continental Breeds— Versatile Dogs

These dogs are also called "do-it-all dogs." Versatile dogs are primarily pointing dogs that show a strong natural desire to retrieve and have had this desire bred into their lines over time. They're called Continental breeds because they originated in Europe, where they are also used to hunt and track furred animals such as hares, rabbits, even wounded deer or stags. Continental dogs are great choices for the hunter who likes to pursue both upland game and waterfowl, but they may need some more specialized training in the retrieving area.

German Shorthaired Pointer. Shorthairs are the most popular of the versatile breeds. They're finding an ever-growing popularity among all types of upland bird hunters, particularly pheasant hunters, because of their strong desire to retrieve and track crippled birds. Shorthairs have docked tails and are grayish with dark chocolate spots covering their entire body, or white with chocolate spots. (In the latter case, they're indistinguishable from a liver-and-white pointer; the shorter tail is the only difference.) They have a very effective pointing instinct, a strong desire to retrieve and a wonderful temperament for the household.

Other Continental Breeds. The German wirehaired pointer resembles a shorthair dog in coloration and its docked tail, but it has a feathery coat and beard. It's also known by its German name, Drathaar. The wirehaired pointing griffon looks like a wirehair, but don't say that to griffon fanatics! The Vizsla is a copper-red color with a docked tail and short hair. Weimaraners are silver-gray with a docked tail and short hair. The Munsterlander looks like an English setter with darker brown or black markings.

The pure pointing breeds may be better pointing dogs than versatile dogs are. And the pure retrievers may be better duck hunters, particularly later in the season—a Lab or golden or Chesapeake coat is designed to withstand the bitter elements experienced in waterfowling; a shorthair's is not. If you're considering a versatile dog to meet both your upland and waterfowl needs, talk your choice over with prospective breeders and locate someone who does both types of hunting with versatile dogs.

Choosing Your Breed

Here's a summary of breed choices to consider, depending on which kind of hunter you are:

• Pure upland hunter: pointing dog; retriever; spaniel. The choice depends on whether you like hunting behind a pointing dog or a flushing dog.

• Pure waterfowl hunter: retriever.

• All-season upland hunter who hunts waterfowl only early in the year or only with friends who have dogs: pointing dog; versatile dog; retriever.

• All-season hunter of both upland birds and waterfowl: versatile dog; one pointing dog and one retriever; retriever.

• Ring-necked pheasant hunter only: versatile dog; retriever; spaniel.

These brief descriptions of the breeds are in no way all there is to say about them. Countless books and magazine articles—and even clubs and organizations—are devoted entirely to one specific breed. After you pick a breed you may want to dive into these resources and learn all you can about the breed's origins, characteristics, health issues and skills.

German shorthaired pointers are an excellent choice for any upland hunter.

German wirehaired pointers can do it all— upland and waterfowl.

Choosing a Breeder

Once you've decided on your breed of choice, it's time to find a breeder. My first advice is that you ignore the ads in the local paper offering free puppies, or puppies for $50, or a pup from any litter without papers. Instead, you should do careful research to find a responsible breeder whose goals are the betterment of the breed and good homes for all of his or her pups. Spending extra money up front for a healthy, sound puppy with an easy-going temperament will be less costly—and less aggravating—in the long run.

With that in mind, don't expect to get the puppy itch, pick up a sporting magazine, find a breeder, make the call and pick up the dog the next day. You should research and choose your breeder well in advance of the date you want the pup. The normal gestation period for dogs is 63 days, and litters are usually planned well in advance. If you want a pup from a planned litter, you may have to put down a deposit before the pups have even been conceived. If you're one of the first to ask, that deposit could get you the pick of the litter, too.

Of course, it's possible to make a fortuitous phone call to a breeder and discover that there is a litter of pups "on the ground" (ready, or nearly ready, to go to homes). Sometimes the pick of the litter has already been taken, and you may be limited in your options; sometimes that limitation may lower the price, particularly if the breeder has a few pups that he or she hasn't been able to sell. Should you be wary of those unsold pups? If you're already certain that you're dealing with a good breeder, there's little cause for concern: Picking the litter is more important than getting the pick *of* the litter.

Most of the time, though, the process of finding a pup is much slower. Start by making a list of breeders to consider. If your hunting buddy has a dog that you think performs well, ask where he got his dog. Check out some of the top sporting dog magazines for listings or look up national breed clubs. The Labrador Retriever Club of America, for example, is the national breed club for Labs. Its website has an online breeder's directory searchable by state. Each listing includes the breeder's contact information, what activities his or her dogs participate in, any titles they have and their health clearances.

Once you've made a list of possibilities, narrow it down by talking with the breeders themselves. Look for one who's breeding dogs for the same things you like to do or the same game you like to hunt. Such a breeder has the same goals you have and, in fact, is breeding dogs to go to people exactly like you.

One way you can be sure about the quality of a breeder is to choose one who offers a written guarantee. Such a guarantee states, loosely, that should the pup be found to be unhealthy—or should it develop certain genetic health disorders—the breeder will offer a replacement pup, a refund or help with the vet bills. The guarantee does not ensure hunting desire or trainability or other factors related to "nurture"; usually, it deals only with inheritable health problems.

James Keldsen, who owns and operates Pine Acre Retrievers in Lakeville, Indiana, and trials and hunts with his Labrador retrievers, says, "The guarantee at least shows that the breeder is willing to stand behind his dogs. It shows a certain amount

Finding the right puppy means doing your homework. Look for breeders who are breeding dogs for the same kinds of hunting you like to do.

of concern for the pups that he produces, and it shows some integrity on his part. Many breeders offer a guarantee only as a means to put in writing their commitment to that puppy and its new owners." While a guarantee can't ensure a stellar hunting dog–that's up to you!–finding a breeder willing to stand behind his or her pups in this way is the most important first step.

Don't be alarmed if you're asked as many questions as you ask the breeder. You should be asked things like what your intentions are for the puppy, how you plan to house the dog, if this is your first dog, whether your family includes children, how much human interaction the puppy will be given, and so on. This information is important to any ethical breeder who prioritizes placing puppies in good, loving homes with owners who will raise and train them to make the most of their abilities. If you have this conversation before you pick your puppy–or if the breeder is several states away–he may even be able to pick out a puppy for you based on your answers and his observations of the litter from day one.

When it comes to price, you probably have a budget. But this is one of the few instances when you really do get what you pay for. Now is not the time to close the purse strings too tightly if you expect to have a healthy, long-lived hunting dog from good bloodlines that trains easily and excels in the field. Throw in a champion pedigree and the price can quickly escalate. Shop around until

BREEDERS

When you've narrowed your list to a few breeders, it's time to make an appointment to see the breeding environment. Pay attention to everything you see, particularly the cleanliness of the kennel operation. Are the adult dogs well cared for? How do they respond to the breeder? The breeder should be able to demonstrate the hunting abilities of your future pup's parents, either through a pedigree or a demonstration in the field. Only expect to see the stud or the dam, though; the breeder may not actually have both parents on hand.

Will the litter be kept inside or outside? A litter kept inside may get more human contact, which is extremely important right from birth if the pup is to be a good house dog. Early human contact will also help at training time. You want a dog that's comfortable around people, and that comfort is imprinted in the early weeks of life. Lots of holding, talking, hugging and playing by the breeder or his family are a definite must.

It is also wise to ask the breeder, should he have the pregnant dam, if he does anything with the puppies before they're born (whelped). The pregnant female should be kept in a very positive environment. Exposing the dam to game can hormonally imprint on the unborn pups. Many breeders introduce the unborn pups to the sound of a gun—safe in their mother's body, they can react to her excitement at hearing the gun.

The breeder must show health certifications and clearances for the parents' hips, eyes and, ideally, hearts. Expect to see X-ray copies of the parents' hips so you can see that there is no hip dysplasia; X-rays aren't necessary if the dog has already been certified by the Orthopedic Foundation for Animals (OFA) or University of Pennsylvania Hip Improvement Program (PennHIP). As many previous generations as possible should be OFA certified. Hips are rated by the OFA as excellent, good, fair or poor; a breeder should not be breeding dogs whose hips are fair or poor. The parents' eyes should be certified against retinal dysplasia and progressive retinal atrophy (PRA) by a veterinary ophthalmologist within the previous year. This is known as Canine Eye Research Foundation (CERF) certification.

The breeder should definitely provide a four- to five-generation pedigree for each parent. The pedigree provides further evidence that the breeder is willing to stand behind his dogs. Look for health certifications with record numbers, and titles the dogs have attained in field, show or obedience work. The designations vary widely and are too numerous to list here, but the breeder will be more than willing to point them out; they are a source of pride to any breeder.

Ask the breeder what materials you'll receive when the pups are born. They should include documentation of shots and deworming; feeding, training and care instructions; an AKC (or other major dog registry) registration card; contacts for local clubs and perhaps information about magazines or books that can help you out.

Picking the right litter is more important than picking a particular puppy from a litter.

you find a good combination of price and documentation of field ability and health clearances.

And finally, ask for references. Good breeders are proud of the pups they've sold in the past. They should be more than willing to give you several names (of non-family members) you can call to ask about their dogs. And if you find that you're happy with your puppy, tell the breeder to keep your name and phone number on file for a future reference for someone else.

Choosing the Puppy

As a general rule of thumb, it's best to choose a pup at around 5 weeks of age. This is when pups really start to become independent and develop personalities. But you won't be able to take the dog home until after 7 weeks. It's better to err on the side of picking the puppy up later than earlier; with a later pickup, very often the breeder will have the puppy separated into his own kennel. Then the dog will already be used to sleeping alone when you take him home. This will make it much easier when you place him in his crate by himself to spend the first night.

Your first decision will be whether to choose a male or a female. If you want to breed your own dog, you'll need to research the subject thoroughly with in-depth references and consultations. If you don't plan to breeed, all males should be neutered and all females spayed. Not only will this help control the dog's sexual urges and cycles, it will reduce the occurrences of certain cancers and health problems, and lead to better overall health.

Just as many stereotypes exist about particular breeds of dogs, the sexes come with theirs, too. According to many people, males may tend to be more aggressive, females a bit more laid back. Males can be high-strung and tough to train; they may need a firm hand, while females may require gentler methods.

But there have been enough exceptions to these generalizations to make them almost obsolete. Your best indicator is the temperaments of the dogs in the pup's pedigree. An easygoing male and female will probably produce like puppies, as will parents with the extreme drive and intensity often found in proven field trial or hunting bloodlines.

When you first see the litter, the pups should be excited to see people and should not cower. Stand back and observe the litter for a few moments. Is there one in particular that hangs back and doesn't get in the mix? Is there one that continually shoves his littermates out of the way? You'll want to stay away from both the overly aggressive puppy and the shy, withdrawn pup hiding in the corner. Look for the one with behavior somewhere in between.

The puppies' coats, teeth, eyes, ears and overall appearance should look healthy, with no evidence of any disease or discharge. Nor should there be any bald spots, apparent sores or evidence of adverse reactions to recent shots.

Narrow your choices to a few pups and take them away from their littermates for a closer inspection. Some may look frightened in new surroundings with new people; they'll want to rush back to the whelping box. Look for the precocious pups that start to explore their new environment. Take a duck wing or a pheasant tail and tease the puppies with it. Some will immediately be fixated on the feathers and chase the tail constantly, even picking it up when you toss it. Other pups won't care one way or the other what you're waving in front of them.

The breeder may also bring out a live pigeon or quail. Pointing dogs with strong instincts may flash into quick sight points, or retrievers may tackle the bird at a full run. The "wing-on-a-string" game that a lot of people play with pointing dog puppies is really nothing more than sight pointing and is not a reliable indication of a pup's future, but any show of bird drive or interest in young dogs is wonderful to see.

You can do some subjective tests to get a feel for the pup's stubbornness or shyness. But sometimes those qualities are brought on simply by the arrival of strangers, or perhaps by something the dogs were doing just before you arrived. Maybe the pups had just been eating, so they are tired and show no interest in you–that doesn't mean that they're all shy or lazy. Or maybe you arrived right at peak playtime and the pups seem uncontrollable. That doesn't mean they will also be uncontrollable during training. But some one-on-one time with the puppies will give you a good feel for their traits; spend an hour or two with them if possible. And don't neglect that gut feeling, either.

One indication of the sensitivity of a dog is to carefully pinch the puppy's toes or ear to see how quickly he'll yip. You won't hurt the dog or leave a mark–it's mere discomfort that the pup is reacting to. A puppy that instantly whines could be a soft dog; another will wonder what the new game is. You could be in for tough negotiations with that one.

When you pick up the puppy in your arms, he should calm down and not continually struggle. He won't stay quiet for long, but a little calmness should be expected. Stay away from the constantly growling or biting pup. Look for the pups–pointing dog or retriever–that like to hold things or carry them around, and those that respond when you clap your hands or whistle. You should be able to entice a youngster to follow you.

When it comes down to it, picking the breeder is the trick, not picking the puppy. Again, *pick the litter, not the pick of the litter.* If you've done your homework thoroughly, checked references, and been impressed with the breeding environment and kennel conditions, then you can just about close your eyes, reach into the box and pick out a pup.

While you're waiting to take the new family member home, use the time to get ready. Buy supplies and make a vet appointment. (You'll probably have an inspection period during which the puppy will need to be examined by a vet in order for you to get your money back should a health problem become evident.) Check back with the breeder to make sure the dog gets his last series of puppy shots, and make an appointment to pick him up. Finally, prepare your household for the invasion.

Take a crate to the breeder's for the puppy's ride home, sign all necessary forms and be sure to get that written guarantee. Ask the breeder if you can call with questions about the bloodline, breeding or the puppy in general. If things have proceeded pleasantly and the dog turns out well, be sure to tell the breeder that you'll give him a good recommendation. You might also get a call from the breeder in a few months–wanting to find out how the pup is training you.

Before the dog is six months old (in most cases), make sure he is registered with the American Kennel Club, United Kennel Club, Field Dog Stud Book or whatever your breeder recommends. You

You've got the right ingredients to start with; now it's time to mold those instincts.

should have received a registration card in your puppy packet–simply fill it out and send it in along with the registration fee. You'll receive a card with some puppy information in a couple of weeks.

Now is the time to consider tattooing your puppy or inserting a microchip under its skin for identification purposes. A dog tattoo is a code that refers to a file in a registry, which often can be accessed on the Internet. A microchip is about the size of a grain of rice and can be inserted between the shoulder blades. It does not have batteries but becomes activated under a scanner. Scanning reveals a code that is listed in a registry and provides information about the dog's breeder and owner, their phone numbers and even the dog's

feeding schedules in some cases. A tattoo or microchip won't fall off like a collar can, and either will provide some level of comfort should your dog get lost. Talk with your veterinarian about the advantages and disadvantages of each method.

From this point forward, it's up to you to stir those pup's genes and mold his instincts so that he'll become the kind of hunting and family dog you desire. The breeder has done his or her part by giving you the best ingredients to work with, and will be interested to hear about the dog's development. In about a year, send the breeder a photo with a little note about how the dog is doing.

But for now, welcome to a whole new world.

CHAPTER THREE

Bringing Your Pup Home

When it comes time to get a hunting dog, we usually have grand dreams of spending days in the woods or on the water with our faithful companion. Stupendous points, fantastic retrieves–our mind's eye focuses on these hunting achievements. Our justification for getting the pooch is almost entirely based on making ourselves a better hunter and enjoying the outdoors more by sharing it with a true friend.

But let's look at this idea carefully. If you don't plan on traveling the world year-round, dog in tow, to find an open hunting season somewhere, and if you don't plan to compete with the dog in a variety of trial or hunt test events, then the actual time the dog will spend hunting pales in comparison to the time he'll spend as a family pal. At home here in Michigan, Josie and Allie earn their keep during the free time I have from work and family from September through December; they spend the rest of the year, and the evenings during the hunting months, racking up a nice bar tab.

So really, this dog you researched and carefully purchased, making darn good and sure of his pedigree and the field ability of his ancestors, will spend most of his time as a loving family dog: playing in the yard, fetching a tennis ball, mooching for dinner and snoring on the couch after a hard day of playing, napping, eating and begging. That's why most of the early training you'll do with your puppy is aimed at developing the dog as a family member and not specifically as a future hunting dog.

Introducing the Puppy to Home and Family

All through the puppy's early training, as he learns his name (which he should be hearing all the time!) and learns to become a new member of the family, your main goal is to end up with a happy, confident dog. Shy, timid, nervous dogs can be difficult to work with. A hunter needs a dog that has some intensity and drive to search out, point, flush and retrieve birds in demanding conditions. In that respect, the stubborn, hard-nosed dog may be easier to work with–you can always tone the drive down a bit, but you can't put it into the dog if it's not there in the first place.

The way you socialize your puppy will go a long way toward developing confidence, which will enhance his natural drive and intensity. Socializing the puppy to all sorts of environments, people and other dogs is perhaps the best thing you can do for his early development. Lots of car rides to new and exciting places will get him used to his travel crate and will teach him that road trips lead to adventures. With supervision (on a checkcord, for example, as described in Chapter Four), let him explore new surroundings where he can't endanger himself. It's a good idea to both let him investigate new surroundings on his own and explore with him: He needs to gain self-confidence, but he also needs to be sure that you'll always be there, too. Always be positive and praise him if he comes back on his own.

Indoors, the house will need to be puppy-proofed

Even though most pups are brought home with intentions of being a hunting machine, they'll end up being around the family more than in the field.

just as it is for a baby. Doors should be latched. Keep anything you don't want chewed or shredded off the floor. Use secure pet gates or baby gates to close off areas where the pup shouldn't go, and hide electrical cords as much as possible. Most important, make sure that kitchen, bathroom and utility-room cabinet doors are secured and that all household toxins, poisons and cleaners are impossible for the pup to reach. You can fill a spray bottle with a foul-tasting substance, such as bitter apple or hot sauce, to spray on the legs of your coffee table or chair in case your dog takes a shine to them.

Just as important as letting your pup explore new surroundings is letting him meet lots of new people. This is another social interaction that needs supervision; be sure to tell the other person how to treat and/or discipline the young pup. If puppy biting is not allowed—and it shouldn't be—inform the pup's new friends and show them how to correct the dog. Encourage them to pet softly, avoid roughhousing, talk nicely to the pup (using his name a lot), pay attention to the puppy when he's calm and say a firm "no" when necessary.

Socializing your puppy to all sorts of people and environments, including some walks in the city, leads to a well-rounded dog that is open to lots of different training scenarios. And if he has confidence that his abilities will help him get along in a variety of situations and trusts that you will always be there to help guide him and to show him these pleasing things, he'll be a willing pupil. Just be sure that consistency is the standard operating procedure. All family members should use the same forms of discipline and maintain the same standard of expected behavior; a checkcord should be used at all times until the pup's responses to commands are reliable; the pup should be praised for good performance; and, especially during these early times of showing your pup a whole new world, you should bring to the task a calm, even, patient temperament.

Socialization—to new places, people and other dogs—lays a good foundation for training.

Becoming the Alpha

That wriggling, squirming, lovable little puppy you just brought home is actually a wolf in dog's clothing—99.8 percent wolf to be genetically accurate. Robert Wayne, an evolutionary biologist from UCLA, discovered this near genetic sameness recently. His work led to the 1993 reclassification of the dog by the American Society of Mammologists and the Smithsonian to (according to the Latin, biological name) *Canis lupus familiaris* from *Canis familiaris*. Wolves are *Canis lupus*, so this reclassification tells us that the dog is simply a subspecies of wolf.

Even though domestication over millennia has brought to the forefront that 0.2 percent that is innately "dog," the wolf isn't very far beneath the surface. One of the dog's wolfish traits is its social structure—that of the pack, led by a dominant, or alpha, male and female. These two eat first and choose the best parts of the kill; they take without challenge from others; they breed first and most; and they lead. They do all these things because they have proven themselves—and not without a fight, either. They earned their alpha status, mostly through aggression.

The first wolves to be domesticated were probably not alphas—assuming that early humans found more use for ten fingers than eight—but the subordinate members of the pack. As subordinates, they were able to accept the leadership of another animal—that is, man—in a new pack. This new pack had a social structure that was very familiar to the wolf: a group of itinerant hunters and scavengers consisting of an alpha male and female and subordinate family members.

Your family is a pack in which every human, including the children, are the alphas to the dog. This doesn't mean you have to wear earth tones and be more assertive and crowd the dog's space,

Your new hunting pal is a subspecies of the wolf, and those wild characteristics aren't far below the surface of his behavior.

but it does mean that your dog needs to listen to you. Each litter has aggressive, alpha dogs—if this is your first pup, you'll want to stay away from these dogs; they'll present challenges that you won't want to deal with. The other pups will have the genes of subordinate dogs and will be more receptive to accepting another as the alpha.

As a member of the pack—and not the leader—the dog will enjoy not having to fend for himself, keep order and maintain discipline. He will know his place and thrive in it. And he'll learn his place based on your actions, which should tell him who's in charge. The most effective way to do this is to communicate in the dog's language, which, remember, is still 99.8 percent wolf.

So how do you do that? Food—the fastest way to a dog's brain—is the best way. Eat your meals first, before putting the dog dish down. Periodically take his food away from him; get down on your hands and knees as he's eating, move your face

into the bowl and pretend to eat. (Caution: You must be very confident that the dog will not bite!) Gradually nudge him out of the way and hoard the food for yourself, pretending to eat it. If he gets close, give a low, throaty growl. If he patiently waits, reward him after a few minutes by giving him his food dish back. This is another indication of your alpha status; if he immediately rushes back in, snatch the food away until he learns to calmly resume eating once you allow him. Make sure all family members except small children do this so that the dog learns that anyone can be around his food. Always praise him for being a good dog when you give him his food back, and pet and stroke him while he eats. This will give him confidence in his decision not to challenge you.

There is to be no aggression on the dog's part at this time. Any sign should be taken seriously, and you may want to contact your breeder or veterinarian if the pup is overtly aggressive around his

The pup should understand that you're the boss and shouldn't put up a fight for food. A dog that knows his role in the family pack is one that will be a joy to train and live with.

food. Now, being aggressive around food with another dog is a different story—in that instance, the two need to sort out who's dominant over whom. But if the dog shows any teeth or growls to his human pack, take away his food for the night. Give it back only when he won't challenge.

Follow the same method with his toys or the place where he likes to sleep. Occasionally take a toy away for yourself and pretend to chew on it or parade in front of him with it; or curl up on his pad, nudging him right off. If he's lying in a doorway that you want to walk through, don't step over him but nudge him with your foot until he gets up and moves out of the way. You are the boss of his life, and the earlier he learns this, the more comfortable he will be. And the better formal training will go because he'll know who's calling the shots.

Another idea is to roll the dog onto his back, take his throat in your mouth and growl until he holds still. This gesture speaks right to the wolf in him— the wolf that just lost a fight for leadership. The growl tells him that all you have to do to end his life is close your mouth; you have won the fight, and you are the one allowing him to survive. That maneuver usually works on the first try. For another lesson, get on all fours with him and put your neck over his, in the dominant position. Be persistent until the dog holds still and accepts you on top; some dogs will even sit and lean their heads back, exposing their throat, which is a classic submissive posture.

Stern growls or tones can convey much to a dog that harsh methods sometimes don't—wolves don't smack one another on the rear end for doing something wrong, but a mother wolf does nip a naughty pup on the ear. Discipline meted out fairly, consistently and firmly (not harshly) will show the dog where his place is in the pack and how he can serve it best. And he'll serve it best by being a willing, happy family member that is a joy to be around— not a stubborn, hardheaded bull that thinks it's his way or the highway. A dog will be much more relaxed if he doesn't have to worry about the burden of pack survival. There will still be challenges— dogs are just like teenagers sometimes—but if you don't give the dog any reason to fear for his survival

or comfort, those challenges should be very few.

All this may sound harsh, but nothing is harder to deal with in training or living with dogs than one that doesn't think you can back up your words, or one that thinks he has you wrapped around his paw and can be a bully. You need to set the pack order right from day one if you're to have any training or hunting success. Your becoming the alpha will also deter the dog from "self-hunting," that is, going off in search of birds with no care of whether you're following or not. Hunting is cooperation, and this cooperation works best with you in charge.

It usually won't take long for the dog to realize he's not in charge, at which point you will probably never have to do any of these things again. You'll be able to step over the dog lying in your path; you won't have to swipe his toys; you won't have to pretend to take his food. Once a dog learns the order of the pack, those lessons are embedded in his brain.

Making the dog clear the way for you helps establish your position in the pack. All communication of your alpha status should be done in language and behavior the dog understands.

Housebreaking

There might be no greater truism with a puppy than this: You'll have to buy a bottle of carpet cleaner and keep plenty of paper towels on hand.

Housebreaking a dog is actually training yourself to recognize the signs that the pup is ready to squat. Dogs learn through repetition—you can't expect them to immediately understand what you mean if they've never been shown what to do. So you have to chain events together for the dog to learn that one event leads to another and warrants a reaction on his part. For the puppy, a full, uncomfortable bladder leads to a squat to relieve the discomfort. You're the one who must show him that the uncomfortable sensation in his bladder first must lead to going outside.

But the dog can't tell you straight out that he has to go, so you need to recognize the signs yourself. Basically, expect your pup to need to go outside after meals, after lots of drinking, after naps, after playing, last thing before bed, in the middle of the night, first thing in the morning, anytime he suddenly becomes uninterested in whatever he was doing and starts exploring, anytime he's frantically whining, or anytime he just can't seem to settle down at a time when he normally does. Those first few weeks, you'll wear out the back door taking him in and out.

So he's showing the signs—now what? Pick him up and tell him, "Outside!" or whatever command will be used for this purpose. Say this command every time he's taken outside to go to the bathroom, and always take him out the same door. Designate a spot in the yard for him to do his business—the smells in that area will cue him into what he needs to do there. As he's going, begin saying, "Hurry up!" or "Go potty!"or a similar cue. Eventually he'll be able to go on that command—a valuable tool for road trips or those times when it's cold outside and he can't seem to find a good spot.

What's that? You missed the signs but not the puddle, and now you're changing your socks? There's not much you can do about that one. Reprimands can only be administered if he's caught in the act. About three seconds after he's done, he's forgotten what he just did—you'll do

If you didn't catch the pup in the act, you missed your chance to teach him where to do his business.

Any attempt to ask to go outside should be rewarded with a trip to the yard.

more harm than good in dragging him back to the scene of the crime. If you catch him during the process, grasp him by the scruff and gently shake, growling a firm "No!" and pointing his nose toward the puddle or pile. Don't smear his nose in it; since hunting dogs make their living at the front end of the body, the nose and mouth should always be about good things. But he should get a snootful so that he learns why you're saying no. Then immediately take him outdoors with an "Outside!" and don't let him come back in until he finishes, goes again or at least makes an attempt to go.

You'll begin to see improvements: Accidents become less frequent, and when they do occur, the puddles or piles are right by the door he's used to exiting. He might begin to whine at the door or scratch; don't tell him to hold it. If he makes any sign that he might need to go out, reward this behavior—this is what he's supposed to do!—by taking him out.

A crate will help with housebreaking; if the pup's area is kept small enough (maybe partitioned off with a divider), the pup will have to either hold it or lie in it—those are the only options. As he realizes that there's only one acceptable place for this business, he'll learn to hold it until he can relieve himself outside and not just when the urge hits.

Crate Training Starts Immediately

In addition to a sturdy collar and leash, a travel crate or kennel is perhaps the most valuable item you can have for your dog. It will be there to aid in housebreaking, to hold the puppy when you leave, to safely transport him anywhere you need to go, and to be a spot where a rambunctious puppy can just go to relax—or to think about his latest misdeed. But what's even more valuable than a crate is a dog that willingly goes into one.

There's no reason for the kennel to be overly large—one big enough for the dog to stand up and turn around in will be sufficient. There are a variety of manufacturers; if you have any plans to take the dog on an airplane, be sure to get one that is airline approved. Most crates disassemble very

easily for cleaning purposes—nothing more than a few latches. If you trust the adult dog not to chew (never trust a puppy not to chew!), kennel pads are available for a little comfort; but until the pup is reliably housebroken, the bare kennel bottom will be easiest to clean.

The dog should view his crate as his den, his bedroom, equivalent to the dens of wild canids. If he appears apprehensive about going inside, try feeding him in the crate with the door left open, or place him inside while he's sleeping. Toss treats for him to run in and gobble; give him a chew toy while he's relaxing inside. Using the crate for travel purposes will show the dog that trips in a crate bring him to whole new worlds to explore. While puppy training, always have the crate accessible with the door open so that the pup can go in and out as he pleases. Pretty soon, you might find the pup searching out his crate as he begins to get drowsy. And every single time you place him inside (or see him going in on his own), say, "Kennel," or whatever command you intend to use.

Everybody says to never use the crate as a form of punishment, and that's very true. However, let's not kid ourselves: There will be times when you

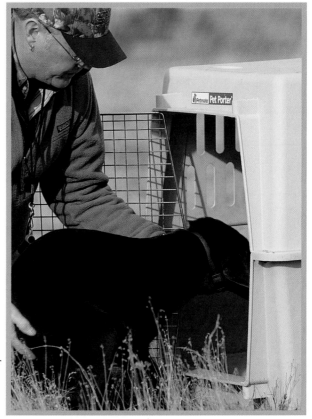

A crate is one of the most valuable pieces of dog equipment you can have: It helps with housebreaking, is the best place for the dog to travel and is his own little den.

need to put the puppy in the slammer for a little peace and quiet or to stop troublemaking in progress. It's like telling a kid, "Go to your room!" Confining the pup to his den will allow him to relax and calm down–and it will give you some time to clean up. If it's necessary to use the crate as a penalty box, make sure he is placed inside with as little emotion as possible. Make your correction and then say, "You know what? Maybe it would be a good idea if you took a little nap in your crate for about an hour," and guide him to his kennel.

You need to steel yourself when it comes to crate training, for this aspect of your dog's education is one of the primary areas where he will learn if he can manipulate you. In short: Never let a barking, whining, howling, screaming, yelping, pleading, cajoling, noisy dog out of his kennel. Professional retriever trainer Charlie Jurney of Beaverdam Kennels in Terrell, North Carolina, says, "My rule was that the dog could not exit the kennel until he stopped barking. Now is the time to train your pup to become a good citizen. Checking on him or taking him out of the crate while he is barking rewards his noisy behavior with your presence. Just

like the crying baby, let him lie. Eventually, he will learn that the only thing he gets from barking is tired." Wait for him to calm down before opening the door.

One of the times this rule is the most difficult to enforce is at night. Jurney encourages, "A dog barking in his crate at 2 a.m. will test your patience; be steadfast." It will be tricky to determine the difference between a puppy that's whining because he has to go to the bathroom and a puppy that's whining because he wants to curl up in your bed. Usually the difference is in degrees of pleading–the bed whine will sound like begging; the bathroom whine will be frantic. You may not recognize the bed whine, but your pup will teach you to recognize the bathroom whine!

This nighttime kenneling is an excellent reinforcement of the lesson to be patient in the crate–and that the crate is a nice place to be. If you plan to allow the adult dog to sleep in the bedroom with you, then bring his puppy crate in there. You'll be able to hear when he has to go outside to relieve himself, and he should be much calmer with you in the room. Again, you will have to harden yourself to his insistent cries for attention, but throwing one of your old shirts in his kennel or placing the crate close to the bed so he can see and smell you will help. Eventually, his crate can be replaced with a soft dog pad or nest–once you're sure he won't get up and mistake the closet for an outhouse.

As I mentioned before, never trust a puppy to not chew anything–puppies just love to explore too much, and they do their exploring with their nose and mouth. Every time you leave for work or the store, put the pup in his kennel. He might begin to scamper away when he hears the car keys jingle, but the kennel is the best place for him. If you can't supervise the young dog, then he should be in his kennel where he can't get into trouble–not only gnawing on your favorite rocking chair, but also getting into poisons or toxins or electrical cords.

Don't leave your pup out alone until he is over a year old, no matter how good he seems on the surface. At five months old, Josie never chewed anything except her toys, and we decided to leave her out of the crate during short trips to the store. A shredded newspaper and shoe were waiting for us

Never trust a pup to not chew on things. In the crate is where he should be while you are away.

one time. Back in the crate she went until she looked trustworthy again three months later—then she chewed up a belt and her dog pad. Once again, crate time for about another three months (she was about a year old at this point). Sure enough, when we left her out again she destroyed a book, two magazines and a houseplant. Eventually, we were able to trust her; she was fine as long as we left the door to our bedroom open and she could sleep on the bed.

The main goal of all this early crate training is to make the dog a good traveler. No matter how long the trip, dogs should always travel inside a kennel that is secured to the vehicle with bungee cords or rope to prevent sliding and tipping—it is the safest place. A patch of black ice on a South Dakota highway during a predawn storm almost turned disastrous for my friend and me one November when we rolled his pickup truck. After we checked with each other for injuries, we scrambled from the upside-down vehicle in a panic for my friend's Labrador. She was in the bed of the vehicle in her crate, which was wedged in beside three sacks of decoys. It hadn't budged, and Tule only got a little dizzy. That crate absolutely saved her life that morning.

"No!"

Besides his name, your puppy will probably hear this word more than anything else. How he reacts to it is up to you: Will he think you're all talk? Or do you have some bite to your bark?

Discipline is a way for the dog, the new pack member, to realize his place in the family. But discipline can take many forms. Though a swift swat on the behind at the time of an infraction does get a point across, so does a low, growling "No!" and maybe a gentle shake of the scruff. If your pup is wandering off and getting into trouble, don't just keep repeating "No!" and hoping the dog will suddenly understand the word. He needs to be shown what "no" means—stop him in his tracks, go pick him up, give a firm "No!" with a shake, and then take him in a new direction and get his attention on something positive. After awhile, he will learn upon hearing that word that it means *Stop what I'm doing and do something else.* How you react when he starts doing that something else will tell him if he was right.

The word "no" might be used most often to stop the puppy from play-biting with those razor-sharp teeth. In this instance, it might be more useful to cry, "Ow!" and act hurt when the puppy playfully bites. More often than not, that will startle the pup, and he'll come back with licks. Never swat a puppy's nose or administer discipline around the mouth. However, you can give an aggressive play-biter a taste of his own medicine by gently curling his top lip underneath a canine tooth and pressing down. This usually needs to be done only once, and if accompanied with an "Ow!" the pup will really begin to understand what that means.

Always follow up a "no" with something positive or steer the pup toward what he should be doing. If he's chewing something he shouldn't, issue the "no" and turn his attention to something he can chew. If his exploration is getting him into trouble, give him the command and then take him somewhere he can explore until his heart's content. Pretty soon, you won't have to physically take him or show him what he should be doing—the "no" command will tell him to stop and try again with something else.

One firm "No!" and then turn the dog's attention to something positive.

Introducing the Puppy to Loud Noises

A gun-shy hunting dog is not very valuable, obviously. While most cases of gun-shyness are hereditary, too many are human-made. Training and gradual introduction are important. Making your pup comfortable around gunfire begins with, very simply, clapping your hands at the puppy's mealtime. The pup will be spooked, to be sure, the first few times he encounters loud bangs, such as cracks of thunder. But he'll take a cue from your reaction. (Some dogs actually never get over the sound of thunder or fireworks but may be fine with the sound of a shotgun.)

All introduction to loud noises should occur only when the dog's attention is focused on doing something he enjoys—eating, chasing a ball, chasing a bird, romping in the yard, wrestling with another dog. Chow time is the best time to begin exposing the pup to loud noises; nothing is better than filling the tummy. Don't sound like a Fourth of July grand finale, but clap one or two times while the dog is nose-deep in his bowl. Don't say anything to the pup or comfort him if he looks spooked; just keep doing whatever you were doing, and soon he'll go back to his food dish and see that there is nothing to worry about. After a couple weeks, slam a cupboard door shut or bang a pan to increase the volume.

During playtime in the house, bang on a wall every now and then and keep right on playing and encouraging the pup to play. The loud noises should become part of the background sounds for the dog instead of distinct events that require a cautious response. Soon, as he begins training for the field, he'll associate these loud noises with birds. After the first few times you shoot a bird, he'll put two and two together and conclude that the gun going off means a mouthful of feathers—as long as you hit what you're aiming at, that is!

Move those noises out into the field, too. This is a good time to use a blank pistol; do not use shotgun blanks at this point. While the pup is running around like a little hooligan, fire off a couple of rounds; if he looks surprised and stops, keep right on walking and encourage him to keep running. Your positive demeanor and body language will be an excellent indicator to the young dog of how to respond to the situation.

Clapping during mealtime is the best way to begin introducing your pup to loud noises. All loud noises should be associated with something the pup enjoys doing—running, playing or eating.

If he can be introduced to some birds at this point, and if he shows great drive toward chasing and inspecting them, start to blend in some loud noises. While next to the pup, helping him inspect the bird, have a partner a good distance off fire the blank pistol once or twice. Only fire it if the pup is very curious, almost aggressive, toward the bird, and don't do it on your pup's first encounters with birds—you want him to experience only one new thing at a time. Some dogs will be very timid when nosing birds, especially live ones, for the first time; now is not the time to shoot off a gun and spook him. Remember: Expose him to gunfire during times that he's doing something he loves.

A word of caution: Do not take the dog to a trap or skeet range in order to expose him to lots of gunfire. The risk is too great, and this is one of the fastest ways to make the dog gun-shy—it's too much too soon, sensory overload where the dog's only logical reaction is withdrawal. The loud noises should be accompanied by something positive and exciting the dog can do—like continuing to eat or chasing a bird—not simply sitting there and listening to the noise.

Introducing the Pup to Water

Even if you have a pointing dog or do not plan to hunt ducks with your dog, every pup should be introduced to water. While some will crash right in without a second thought, most will be apprehensive in their first contact. Make sure the water is warm—at least around 60°F—before introducing a very young pup to it.

The best course is to have your pup go into the water on his own with your encouragement. He'll probably splash around in the shallows without a care in the world—as long as his feet are touching bottom, he's fine—and if you make it fun by letting him chase and fetch a favorite toy, he won't even notice he's in the water. Eventually, he'll wade out to chest-deep water; then he'll probably bounce back and forth and bark, unable to make the leap into swim-depth water.

So climb in there with him. Put on some knee-high boots or waders and trudge out there, clapping your hands or enticing him with a favorite fetch object. He'll probably continue to run back

Don't rush your pup's introduction to water. Let him explore the shallow water; taking his favorite bumper along will help him feel comfortable in deeper and deeper levels.

and forth and bark at you to come back and play with him, but just keep tempting him. In those first few daring paddles he'll look like a carp out of water, but he'll smooth out. Give him a reward by letting him fetch his toy or puppy bumper, and direct him back to shore. After that, try standing on shore and tossing his toy into deeper and deeper water until he must swim on his own to get it. Keep everything positive; do not comfort the frightened dog lest he think that he is right in feeling scared. The strategy is much like what you did when introducing him to loud noises.

What if the pup still won't swim out on his own? Try taking him out there with you while you swim or wade into water deep enough that he has to swim. Gently ease him into the water on his own, pointed toward shore—which he will make a beeline for—and let him paddle for a few seconds. Again, always keep it fun; do not just toss a novice youngster over the side of a canoe and expect him to like it. But some pups may require a gentle nudge to get their feet paddling—and then they'll see that as long as those legs keep moving, they'll be just fine.

Early Training with Basic Commands

Although it is way too early to expect any sort of reliability of response to commands, you can start to introduce your pup to his "vocabulary" whenever the opportunity presents itself. Don't pass up the chance to identify a correct behavior with the name you intend to give it. If you can easily get your pup to come to you while whistling or clapping, you can start saying, "Come!" when he's on his way. If the dog is a natural sitter, be ready for those times when it looks as if he's getting ready to sit; say the command as he's dropping his rear. Or hold his food dish high and move it back over his head; his momentum will force him to sit. Say the command when he looks as if he's headed in the right direction, praise him and give him his food.

While you're not really training in these instances, you are laying groundwork for formal training. This early exposure to the words you'll use to communicate with your dog for the rest of his life will make those words familiar to him once you start his lessons. Then you'll be showing him the correct behavior—and that he must do it when you say so and not just when he feels like it. There are lots of reasons humans decided to domesticate dogs instead of hippos, one of them being that dogs are intelligent animals that, with repetition and fairness, can amass quite a vocabulary. It never hurts to begin his ABCs if he's doing things right anyway.

The Outside Dog

If you plan to house your dog outside, you'll still want to keep him indoors as a puppy—you shouldn't let him stay out in his own kennel while he is very young. And you'll still want to give him plenty of housetraining for those times when you may want to bring him in, either because of extreme weather or because you want him to keep your feet warm.

An outdoor dog shelter—or an outdoor kennel for the dog to use as his restroom or to enjoy a nice spring day—must have fencing, flooring, shade, water,

Hold his food dish above his head and slowly move it back. That should force his rump down—a good time to introduce the "sit" command.

Fencing, flooring, shade, water, space and shelter—things to consider if your dog is to live outside.

room to get a little exercise and a doghouse. The doghouse will, of course, be necessary only if the dog remains outside at night; you won't need one if the dog always stays indoors at night.

The fencing should be at least 6 feet high, and the gate should be locked to discourage dognapping. Water should be available at all times; a pail with the handle clipped to chain-link fencing will prevent the bucket from being tipped over. In the winter, you may need to switch to an electronic water system to keep the ice off. For shade, if there aren't any nearby trees, kennel canopies are available.

Flooring should be concrete or rock gravel; the best option is rubber or vinyl mesh flooring, usually sold in interlocking squares, made especially for outside kennels. The squares sit off the ground a bit to let air circulate so they won't heat up, and the mesh allows liquid waste to run right through.

A raised, flat section of flooring will give the dog a nice area to lie down. Your best bet is to get your hands on a good dog-supply catalog and comb the section on outside kennel supplies.

Don't neglect to watch the local news for notices about dangers to pets from extreme weather. Even if you have to confine your dog to the basement, he'll be better off than he would be toughing out the weather. Dogs may be virtually identical to wolves in terms of genetics, but their domestication didn't help much in maintaining the physiological and behavioral traits that allow wolves to survive in the wild.

A warm, workable, mutually satisfactory relationship with your hunting dog starts when he's a pup. That bond is based upon him learning how things work in the human world—and he'll learn that you are his friend who also happens to be in charge.

CHAPTER FOUR

Training Equipment

The money we spend purchasing our dog and keeping him healthy and well fed–not to mention the Christmas stocking we'll fill with dog biscuits and toys every year–aren't the only times our wallet takes a hit. The dog's training and hunting equipment can rival our own in expense as well as in the space each takes up in the closet. While it isn't imperative to have every single one of the following items to train your dog to bust the brush or churn up the water after birds, they can make life easier and present more training options. Almost all of this equipment can be used for training either a pointing dog or retriever; equipment specific to one type of dog is noted.

Collar

The fact that your dog should always be wearing a collar while training goes without saying. A collar gives you a point of contact and some leverage if you have to manipulate the dog in some way. And of course, you can clip a leash to the collar for walking your pupil to and from training grounds if

there are any hazards nearby, such as a busy road.

But you may not always want a collar on your hunting dog, particularly a retriever, and most especially when it comes to waterfowl hunting. If you're duck hunting in heavy brush, the collar can hang the dog up. A situation that was once thrilling (seeing your dog retrieve a bird) can quickly become treacherous (having to rescue him).

For now, let's focus on training. Collars come in all sorts of shapes, sizes and colors–upland hunters usually prefer blaze orange on their dogs. The buckle-type collars are stronger than those that snap together, which can rip apart if the dog is really struggling against a cord. These two, though, are both standard collars, and you'll probably have one on the dog at all times, even around the house.

Other training collars are the pinch collar or the slide collar (sometimes called a choke collar). The pinch collar has dulled metal spikes on the inner surface. When the collar is pulled taut, the spikes extend into the dog's neck, causing discomfort. Usually this discomfort stops naughty behavior

One of the best ways to communicate to your dog is through pressure around the neck with different types of collars: regular pet collar (left), slide or choke collar (center), pinch collar (right).

A bumper is the mainstay of most training sessions.

A leash is a necessity for everyday life, whether on a walk with the family or training.

immediately; when the collar relaxes, the spikes lay flat. The slide collar works in the same fashion but has no spikes; its constriction around the dog's neck causes the discomfort.

With pinch and slide collars, you should use small tugs and releases instead of constant pressure, which can injure the dog. Some trainers refer to these as "pop" collars, because you pop the dog and then immediately release. Both collars are very humane ways of teaching and can get through to a particularly stubborn dog when other collars or other methods of instruction won't.

A brass plate or tag should be affixed to all collars, labeled with contact information in case the dog runs off. I highly recommend that you do not put your dog's name on the collar, but instead, simply the word "REWARD." If a person finds your dog and learns his name, it's a small leap to dognapping, but the offer of a reward is a great encouragement to return the animal. Also, if your dog is identified with a microchip or tattoo, indicate this on the tag so that the code can be located.

Electronic collars are a complex subject. They're covered separately toward the end of this chapter.

Leash and Checkcord

A leash is a necessity for every dog; one nice model incorporates a slip collar at the end for a complete training item. Retractable leashes can be useful for daily walks, but their selling point—the ability to put the brakes on the dog with the push of a button—can actually encourage the dog to pull harder against the steady resistance.

A checkcord is a valuable piece of equipment every trainer should have. This long piece of rope (20 to 60 feet or longer) is attached to the dog's collar. Checkcords are very simple to make, or you can buy one that will move through brush easily; the stiffer the rope, the easier it seems to slide through cover. All pups should have a checkcord attached for their first forays afield. It allows you to gain control of the dog; you can step on it to slow a dog down or stop him should he be headed for danger—or if he's not listening. With a checkcord, you can also teach a pup to

A long checkcord can allow the dog to be farther away but still gives you some control.

quarter a field (move back and forth in a zigzag pattern questing for birds). The rope will slither through the brush and, surprisingly, will hang up very rarely.

Whistle

The whistle is another extremely valuable training tool, and you should always have one around your neck. At great distances, the dog will not be able to hear your voice; a high-pitched whistle will carry through wind and waves and woods. Most hunting dogs are trained to sit and/or come to a whistle, and there may be no more useful commands than these two in preventing the dog from becoming lost and keeping him out of harm's way. And sometimes a dog will listen much better to the whistle than to spoken commands.

You may look through a sporting dog supply catalog and wonder where to begin when you see all the different whistles available. The good news is that you really can't go wrong with just about any of them; just stay away from silent whistles, which are very limited in their range. You'll want a whistle, pea or pealess, that you can blow a good sharp blast through and that you can also trill. The tone and cadence of your whistle blasts will mean different commands to the dog.

Crate

As mentioned in the previous chapter, the travel crate is perhaps one of the most valuable training items. A crate is the best, safest place for the dog to ride to and from hunting and training grounds; crate training around your home can also teach some canine patience and will keep the dog out of trouble.

Training Pistol

A good blank pistol is vital to teach the dog to associate great things with the sound of the gun. As detailed in the previous chapter, the dog should experience only positive things while hearing a gun go off. Different pistols hold different caliber cartridges of blank shells, and you'll eventually want to graduate to blank shotgun loads.

A blank training pistol provides a gradual escalation in the sound of gunfire and teaches your dog that a gunshot is a good thing (above). Almost any whistle will do the job—it's your choice (above left).

Bumper

You can't make a good retriever without bumpers, oblong training tools designed to be fetched and carried in a dog's mouth. Basic bumpers are either canvas or plastic with small knobs. While canvas bumpers hold scent better; plastic ones last longer and retain their color better. You can also attach streamers or scent bands to either type of bumper to make it more versatile and visible.

You should have several bumpers in a variety of types and colors. Most people use white bumpers for *marks* (retrieves where the dog sees the object being thrown). Blaze orange, which is nearly invisible to canines, works well for *blind retrieves* (those where the dog does not see the bumper). The blaze orange helps you locate the bumper should your dog not be able to. You can also buy camouflage, black, yellow, green and dual-tone bumpers. A mesh bag is handy for keeping bumpers together and toting them to and from the field.

One of the most popular retrieving items on the market today is the Dokken Dead Fowl Trainer. These trainers are excellent fetching tools that are shaped—and weighted—just like real birds. They have a hard plastic head that hangs limply from a string to discourage the dog from shaking the bumper, and the body is made of a rubbery-foam material that feels amazingly like a bird and can be injected with scent. Dead Fowls ride low in the water, just like a real bird. They come in many different bird species—from big geese to small mourning dove models, which are suitable for puppies. The only problem with Dead Fowls is that they can be difficult to throw very far, particularly when they become waterlogged; but if you use one with a launcher, your problem is solved. Definitely have at least one or two in your arsenal; some dogs develop a fondness for them.

Small dumbbell-shaped bumpers are made specifically for *force-fetching* (training the dog to pick up an object and hold it on command). The dumbbell shape makes it easier for the dog to pick the bumper up off the ground and hold the bumper in the middle.

The Dokken Dead Fowl Trainers provide a realistic feel in the dog's mouth (left). Bumpers come in several shapes, sizes and colors (above).

Scent

Bottled scent–grouse, pheasant, quail, duck–is put on bumpers and sprinkled in areas where birds might be to increase the scenting conditions. You can also use it to leave a trail to train upland flushing dogs to keep their noses to the ground in following a track to the bird. Other scent–such as deer–can be used in a deterrent fashion to break the dog of chasing undesired game.

Bell or Beeper

You can use these two pieces of equipment to keep track of your dog's location while upland hunting. The old-fashioned bell–which comes in a wide variety of shapes and tones, usually the size of a small cowbell–will fall silent when a pointing dog goes on point. For some,

The sound of the bell is for you, not the dog, so pick one you like.

using this type of bell is the traditional way to hunt, and memories of upland hunts always have a soundtrack of a tinkling or clanging bell.

The more high-tech method is to use a battery-operated beeper collar. Most have a variety of tones or modes; you can program the collar to emit different cadences of beeps so you can follow multiple dogs–each one will be unique. For example, one mode beeps every 5 seconds while the dog is running, with a succession of quick beeps when the dog is on point. Some modes are silent while the dog is running and beep only when the dog stops. Others fall in between, beeping every 10 seconds while the dog's moving, with rapid beeps to signal a point. Most beeper collars also come with a "locate" function, in which the beeper sounds when a button on the transmitter you carry is pushed.

Beepers come in many styles and models. They all do one thing: locate your dog in the field.

If you have a close-working flushing dog that never gets turned around or out of sight, you may not need a beeper. Most experienced pointing dog owners these days have one on their dogs because they want their dogs to range far and wide in search of birds; with a beeper collar, the dog can be out of sight on point and still be easily found.

Dog Boots

In hot, prickly environments such as the Southwest, dog boots can save a hunting dog's pads from becoming bloody. Lots of different shapes, sizes and materials are available–leather, neoprene, Cordura, etc.–and you can even make your own with cotton wrap and duct tape. There probably isn't a dog alive that truly likes to wear boots, but they can be a lifesaver, particularly on the front end of a multiple-day hunting trip. Boots made of neoprene with rubber gripper soles are great for hunting in the snow–they prevent slippage and keep snow from accumulating between the dog's toes.

Using a bird launcher will make sure your dog won't catch the bird as it's released.

A dummy launcher can put some more distance—and more challenge—on your dog's retrieves.

Dog Vest

For waterfowl retrievers that work in nasty, late-season conditions, neoprene dog vests can add a measure of warmth while the dog sits and waits for birds. Pointing dogs can wear a blaze-orange vest fitted on the underside to prevent the dog's belly from getting beaten up by brush. The blaze orange also helps with visibility—consider a white dog hunting in snow or a dark dog hunting in autumn woods.

Bird and Dummy Launchers

Though you may find you don't need either of these items, they're fun to have and can greatly improve the training scenarios you're able to design. They can be expensive, however; some people prefer to spend any extra training money on birds to really excite the dog.

Bird launchers are cages—mostly electronic nowadays—that hold a bird until a release button on a remote transmitter is pushed. The bird sits on a piece of tough material that folds over the top of its head; this material is secured with a lever. When the release button is pushed, the lever whips back. Powerful springs pull the material taut, propelling the bird skyward, where it takes flight. This type of launcher is useful for teaching a pointing dog to remain steady once scent is detected. Some pointing dogs will "creep" on point and crowd the bird, perhaps even attempting to catch it on the ground. With a bird launcher, you can release the bird as soon as the dog, once steady, takes a cautious step closer. This tells him that as soon as he scents the bird, he must remain still; otherwise the bird will escape.

Dummy launchers shoot retrieving bumpers a considerable distance. They come in two basic models, handheld and stationary. Handheld launchers can propel smaller fetch objects around 200 to 300 feet; the launch is accompanied by the firing of a blank cartridge. The jolt a handheld launcher gives your arm is pretty powerful, so some companies have designed stock mounts, allowing you to hold the launcher like a shotgun. These launchers are not that expensive and are an excellent method for increasing the distance of retrieves.

Stationary launchers can throw birds or even Dokken Dead Fowls about 40 to 50 yards, very high in the air. These launchers are used most often by competitors in training their dogs for trials and hunt tests. They're positioned out in the field and manned by a "bird boy." Some are remote controlled, while others are manual. Stationary launchers can be very expensive. If you plan on just hunting with your dog, you can get away without one, but you'll find a portable, handheld launcher very useful in your training exercises.

Backing Dog

Used almost exclusively for pointing dogs, these wooden cutout dogs are employed to teach a dog to "honor" or "back" another dog's point. When two pointing dogs hunt together, it is something of a social error for one dog to steal another's point. A backing dog teaches the honoring dog to stop solidly at the sight of another dog on point. When dogs are highly trained in this skill, it's exciting to see multiple dogs lined up across the landscape; you can follow the sight of one to find the next, all the way to the dog that has the birds pointed. Some people who hunt retrievers and pointing dogs together use backing dogs to teach their retrievers to sit at the sight of a pointing dog in honor of the dog's point.

Birds

A popular saying is that "it takes birds to make a bird dog." Pigeons, quail, pheasants, ducks, chukars–lots of different birds can be used to get a dog, and especially a young pup, exposure to live birds. Nothing brings out the drive and intensity in a young dog like live game. With puppies, stick with quail or young chukars–pheasants or ducks can be aggressive and can scare a pup. To find a place to buy birds for training, check around at local retriever or pointing dog clubs or shooting preserves. But first make sure you know the dog-training rules in your state; they're available through your state's wildlife agency.

You can usually get pigeons for free if you find a farmer who agrees to let you trap some. Most dog-supply catalogs sell equipment to help in this adventure, or to aid in housing birds for future training. For some great retriever training, find a farmer who will allow you to shoot the pigeons dirtying up his farmyard–but be sure to hunt and shoot only where he says you can. A couple afternoons of shooting pigeons as they flap around a farmer's stubble field may be all it takes to give a retriever an idea of what the hunt is all about. This kind of training also allows you to work on all phases of the dog's hunting repertoire: sitting patiently, being steady, waiting for shots and taking signals to the downed bird.

Electronic backing dogs are vital in teaching your dog to honor another's point.

Electronic Collar

Few subjects are as contentious among hunting-dog owners as the debate over the merits of electronic collars. In their infancy, many years ago, e-collars were called "shock" collars because that's all they did to the dog—they delivered one intense electric stimulation. Fortunately, e-collars have advanced by such leaps and bounds as to make those bad memories moot. Now they have variable intensity levels, administering anything from a vibration (called a "pager" on some collars) to a high-intensity volt to stop a dog from getting into a potentially life-threatening situation, such as running onto a busy road or picking a fight with a rattlesnake.

Features. You can't go wrong with any of the major e-collar manufacturers; prices can run high, but your money will be well spent. Some of the basic features to consider are the battery, the transmitter and receiver, the range, and the levels and delivery of stimulation.

Most collars have rechargeable batteries; one charge can last through several hunts. A flashing light indicates when the battery is in need of recharging. Some collars have replaceable batteries, a nice option. If a battery goes low while you're hunting, you can replace it and have a fully functional collar immediately—provided you remembered to bring an extra battery.

Transmitters (the part you hold) and receivers (the part around the dog's neck) vary widely among manufacturers and models. Some transmitters can control multiple collars and even other electronic equipment such as beepers, backing dogs or bird launchers. But the trend with transmitters has been toward smaller and more waterproof. Most can fit in a specially designed holster, on a belt clip, or on a lanyard around your neck. Receivers are also becoming smaller, but some still have short, durable antennas that increase range and reliability.

Range varies among models. More expensive models have added features and increased range. For retriever owners, a range of around a half-mile is usually more than sufficient; you need a flushing retriever close in the uplands if you want to get a shot. And for waterfowl hunting, if a retrieve is longer than a quarter-mile, you'll probably want to go to the bird with the dog, either on foot or in a boat. About a mile is a good range for pointing dogs, which can venture far and wide in search of game.

For the most part, stimulation is delivered in one of two modes. With "continuous" stimulation, the impulse continues as long as you hold the button down, with an emergency shutoff after 8 to 10 seconds. A "nick" or "momentary" impulse works just like it sounds; this extremely brief impulse is delivered only once, even if you keep holding down the button.

Levels of stimulation vary from modest impulses to hard jolts meant solely to save a dog's life. If you're unsure of whether an impulse will hurt the dog, I urge you to try it on yourself—no kidding! Before I put a collar on my dog, I press the probes into the meat of my palm and try the level that I normally use to correct my dogs to make sure the collar is working properly. You'd be amazed at how slight the impulse really is—it feels like nothing more than a small pinprick, sometimes just a vibration.

Many professional trainers say that one thing that continues to give people the wrong impression about e-collars is that somewhere along the line, companies started calling them "electronic trainers." Almost every single professional trainer I have spoken with says that you do not "train" a dog with an e-collar; rather, it is a training aid to help you in your teaching.

Usage. The basic premise behind e-collars is twofold: First, deliver the minimum amount of stimulation that gets a response from the dog. This response may be as subtle as a twitch of an ear, so watch closely. Then adjust the stimulation from that starting point to achieve the desired response, which is the obedience of a command.

This method works most effectively if you keep the second premise in mind: The dog should think that he has total control of the collar. This is one of the nice things about e-collars; the dog assumes responsibility for his own behavior. His noncompliance to a command turned the collar on, and his compliance turned it off. Sometimes, a nick is all that is needed as a reminder to do the right thing once the dog knows what that right thing is.

For example, if the dog knows the "come" command reliably while on a checkcord or in the yard but goes brain dead in the field, the e-collar can be an effective tool if the dog knows how to respond to it. The proper way to get the right response is to turn off the stimulation as soon as the dog makes the first positive sign toward obeying. If the dog is ignoring the "come" command and streaking away from you, push the continuous button, which will usually stop the dog. He'll begin to turn. As soon as he turns toward you, release the button and encourage the dog to come by whistling, clapping, calling his name and repeating the command, all while acting as if nothing has happened.

After a half-dozen repetitions, the dog will learn that, should he ignore the command, this prickling discomfort will start in his neck and will be relieved only when he obeys a command that he knows. After that, a nick from the collar at the noncompliance will be the only brief reminder that he'll need; you won't need to hold down the continuous button.

Retriever trainer Mike Lardy has probably done more for developing and honing of e-collar training than anyone. His videos on the subject of collar conditioning should be on your shelf (see the Appendix). Almost all e-collars now come with instructional videos, which are extremely valuable tools in helping you train your dog correctly from the beginning. Such videos have much more detailed information about training specific commands with an e-collar than this book has. In fact, I would recommend that you consider only collars that come with an instructional video.

I had been dead set against using an e-collar on Allie, my setter; I figured that dogs had been trained for ages without e-collars. I could handle it–no problem. Then I found myself chasing the six-month-old down for the fifth time as she ran away in pursuit of robins that kept flitting in front of her nose. There I was, making dive after dive at her trailing checkcord, landing in the mud (and I was visiting my future in-laws at the time). I'd finally catch up to her as she bolted into the road.

The modern electronic collar—with its many levels of intensity, nonstimulation modes and range— has been a savior for many trainers. Used properly, they are one of the most humane training aids.

At last I said, "That's it. I've had it. I'm tired of chasing her and dealing with her when I finally catch her." So I went to the e-collar. In the first session, after about five impulses when she disobeyed my "come" command, she was bolting back to me at my slightest whistle to hunt closer. I was a convert.

And that's basically what an electronic collar is—nothing more than a cordless checkcord, a long-distance tap on the shoulder or a hearing aid, as my dad says. It reminds the dog, "Hey! Remember me? The guy who feeds you? I'm still watching you!" Some dogs will become "collar wise," meaning that they behave perfectly as long as the collar is around their neck and become delinquents when it is off. While you can cure this problem with more repetition and training with the collar off, I say who cares if you have to put the collar on for hunting or training? For my dogs, the e-collar is their hunting collar, and they go berserk when I pull it out and show it to them. They know it's time for business, and they're going to get to run or fetch.

When it comes down to it, the e-collar provides the trainer with a way to administer a correction to a dog without having to catch and corral him first, at which point he may have forgotten why he's being corrected. It helps to take the emotion out of training—indeed, if we have a temper while using an e-collar, then it can and will be an abusive tool. The collar helps us keep that level head because the correction is instantaneous, administered at precisely the right moment to speed training and help the dog make the proper connection.

As I mentioned in Chapter One, too often amateur trainers react to a dog's noncompliance to a command by flying off the handle. Then they have to worry about both training the dog to execute the command and bringing the dog's confidence back up. Toss in having to catch the dog first, perhaps chasing him into the next county, and that temper can quickly blow steam out our ears. With an e-collar, the correction occurs immediately and at a level the dog understands and can effectively respond to.

Home Alternatives. Two other types of electronic collars are for use around the yard—those that go with an invisible fence and bark collars. The invisible fence is usually a boom or bust situation—a dog either responds extremely well to it or bolts across the line, sucking it up and taking the juice. The dog may then actually be prevented from getting back into the yard as he approaches it from the outside. In my opinion, a fenced-in yard is a much better option.

Bark collars can deliver stimulation when the dog vocalizes or can even spray a mist in the dog's face. These are popular if you live in a neighborhood or subdivision and you have a nuisance barker; more training with a "quiet" command can accomplish the same goal and save some money.

Helpers

Having a friend or two for assistance can make all the difference in the world. If your buddy has a new dog, too, think about setting up some regular training sessions. Helpers can be stationed far out in a field to throw bumpers, or they can shoot birds while you work a young pointing dog. An extra pair of hands to perform other aspects of the training exercises will allow you to focus entirely on your dog and the lesson at hand.

WHERE TO BUY EQUIPMENT

Though there are several dog-supply catalog companies, some of the more popular ones are listed below. They carry just about all the gear you could ever want to buy—and then some!
• Cabela's, www.cabelas.com, 800-742-4008 (for catalog request)
• Dobbs Training Center, www.dobbsdogs.com, 888-326-5527
• Dogs Afield, www.dogsafield.com, 800-863-3647
• Lion Country Supply, www.lcsupply.com, 800-662-5202

Having a helper will allow you to set up any type of training scenario imaginable.

CHAPTER FIVE

Basic Obedience Training

In short order, that wriggling bundle of fluff you brought home will not only become attached to the family, he'll also be growing into his gangly ears and legs. You won't be able to imagine your life without this new best pal, but his misbehavior will have gotten old and, well, hunting season always seems just around the corner.

Some folks say that you should let a dog be a dog—with no type of training whatsoever—for nearly a year before beginning formal training, and some don't encourage formal training at all. I'm not in that camp. Basic obedience training is fun, and for the dog that is also to fulfill a role as a family member in the house, it's necessary. In my opinion, basic training makes specialized training for hunting easier because it gives the dog a foundation, a language he can understand to fall back on and a positive note he can end on if everything else is failing. A dog that has small things he can be successful at will be more confident in new situations and environments.

Further, nearly all training situations for hunting begin with some sort of an obedience command. A retriever expected to line a difficult blind retrieve must first "sit" and "stay." A pointing dog expected to quarter based on the pressure administered from a checkcord must first know what that pressure means, which is taught with the "come" or "heel" commands. And it's vital to have a well-controlled dog around vehicles or other hunters both before and after the hunt.

Genes and bloodlines have endowed your dog with drive and skills, the raw ingredients of a hunter. It takes training, experience afield and obedience to mold that drive and hone those skills. When a pup is around 12 to 16 weeks, it's a good idea to start teaching him the commands that will

be the foundation for everything he'll do—both in the field and around the home—until a gray muzzle and arthritic joints earn him the right to ignore us. Like all mammals, a dog learns and retains best while it's growing and developing; this is why we send kids to school young, and it's why we can't teach an old dog new tricks. (Well, we can; it's just easier when the dog is young.)

If a spouse or someone else will be with the dog for a significant amount of time each day, it's a good idea for both of you to work on these basic obedience commands with the dog—but work on them separately. Make sure that you both give and enforce the commands in the same way and that your praise is equal, too. If one of you gives treats and the other only verbal praise, it's not going to take a genius to figure out which one the dog will respond to better.

It's best to limit obedience training to a couple of 10- to 15-minute sessions per day, usually in the morning and evening. Short, fun sessions teach more than long battles of will.

For basic obedience commands, start with a regular collar, a leash, a 20-foot checkcord (something akin to cloth clothesline will work just fine), a whistle and the dog's crate. You may choose to use a slide collar or pinch collar, but not on a really young puppy. First try to teach these commands without much pressure. If you have a stubborn ox—or one that picks up the commands very quickly and then refuses to obey after a time—then it might be a good idea to switch to a slide collar or pinch collar. Just remember not to apply steady, constant pressure with these collars, because they could cause injury. Rather, the pressure should come in light "taps"—on, off, on, off; tug, release, tug, release—to administer the discomfort necessary to get the proper response.

Basic obedience training lays a solid foundation for more advanced training and is vital for the house dog as well as the hunting dog.

The pressure points behind the dog's ears are the perfect places for effective communication.

Rewards, Praise and Discipline

For a very young puppy, and anytime you start out in obedience training, treats are a great way to get through to a dog. But you'll eventually want the dog to respond to your commands because he's trained to—not because he's expecting some free eats. As soon as possible, start phasing out treat rewards, perhaps giving them every third or fifth or seventh time the dog performs the command correctly.

When you don't treat, praise with a nice tone, a rub on the dog's shoulder and a "Good boy!" Don't go overboard—you don't want the dog to start acting foolish in response to clownish praise. He must not think that it's okay to begin horsing around or that the lesson is over. Calm praise will lead to a calm dog that can accept and, more importantly, understand that praise. Look for laid-back ears and a "doggy smile," perhaps a lick of the chops or a swallow as an indication that he knows he's been a good boy and that you are giving him a verbal and physical reward.

Not all behaviors warrant praise, of course. Miscues will occur throughout the learning process as the dog tries to figure out just exactly what you're asking. In those cases, stop the dog, take him back to the beginning and start the command again. But some miscues will be blatant refusals and ignoring of your commands, commands that you know he knows. Dogs enter—and pass through, thankfully—an equivalent of the "teenage" years and the typical streaks of rebelliousness that come with them. During that time, some recourse will be necessary.

Actually, the same rule applies to the use of regular collars as well—a constant pull will only encourage the same in the puppy. Do not use an electronic collar to teach obedience commands; that type of collar is used for reinforcement once the dog learns the commands conventionally, should you choose to go that route.

The placement of the collar on the dog's neck goes a long way toward effective communication with him through the leash or checkcord. There are special tools designed to fit snugly around the dog's neck at the proper pressure points. One is called the Command Lead and is employed by well-known pointing dog trainer Rick Smith; retriever trainer Charlie Jurney uses his variation, called the EZ Lead. For such a collar to work properly, it should be positioned in the groove just behind the dog's ears. A small amount of pressure applied at this point will get the dog's attention—and short taps will tighten and release the lead, the release being the reward. These collars work like a slide collar and a leash all in one.

According to pointing dog trainers Rick Smith and Sharon Potter, "The lead and the restriction of it teaches our dogs to tune in to us and go along with us at any speed in any direction. The dog learns to pay attention and take direction from the person holding the lead, which eventually transfers to the dog going with us off lead via watching the body language it learned while on the lead."

You want a well-behaved, upstanding citizen in the house and field, and sometimes, you'll need to administer a little reminder of your alpha status to the dog. This is not being cruel. Some would argue that letting a dog become an all-around ruffian is cruel; it can lead to him running into traffic because he won't come, getting in a dogfight because he won't sit or stay, scaring neighbors or kids on a walk because he won't heel and making a complete catastrophe of your Christmas party because he won't lie down. Sometimes discipline is necessary—but remember to always follow any form of discipline with a command the dog can perform well, and end with praise.

If you find that you need to administer discipline, you should follow the same philosophy employed by trainers who use the electronic collar: Use the mildest form that gets the desired response from your dog. It may take awhile to find the form of discipline that gets through to a particular dog; that's why some trainers choose the electronic collar—it delivers a consistent, fair form of correction that the dog readily understands. (I would argue that the e-collar is *not* used for discipline; there's a big difference between correction and discipline.) Indeed, the e-collar tends to get rid of the need for discipline per se, as it gives the trainer the ability to stop (correct) the dog before the bad behavior can continue. Once the behavior is corrected, there's no need to administer a punishment (discipline).

The e-collar aside, some effective forms of discipline include a swat on the rump, a bite on the ear (which is how Mom kept the litter of pups in line when they were very young) or simply a stern voice and a growl. Some dogs are softies, and you'll find that all you have to do is wag your finger at them and they'll get the idea that they were being a hoodlum. Others will look at us as though to say, *Is that the best you can do?* Especially hardheaded dogs might require the assistance of a professional trainer.

I consider the word "no" not a form of discipline but rather a command that means "stop what you're doing right now." If your dog understands this command well—and can the follow your direction to change his behavior to something constructive rather than destructive—you may find that you won't need to discipline the dog very much.

Sit

"Sit" is usually the first—and easiest—command to teach a pup. It's even easier if the puppy is a natural sitter, which some dogs seem to be. In that case, you'll start to recognize when the dog is about to sit; time the command so that he hears it just before his rump starts down.

Another easy way to get a dog to sit without any physical manipulation is with his food dish—hold it high over his head and gradually move it back toward his rear. He'll follow it with his head, moving farther and farther back until it forces his bottom

to the ground. Tie in the command as his bottom is moving down.

In teaching "sit," I like to use the "pull-up-push-down" maneuver. Very simply, with a leash on the dog's collar, gently pull up on the leash as you push down on his rump. Having control of the dog on both ends will also help you guide him into a straight sit. Sometimes, particularly with retrievers, a sloppy sit—where the dog sits sort of "sidesaddle"—can lead to handling difficulties because the dog is not properly aligned. The sooner the dog develops proper habits, such as straight sits, the easier handling will be.

As you push the dog's rump down, say clearly—and only once—"Sit." Once he's on the ground, praise with either a treat or a stroke of the shoulders, use the leash to get the dog back on his feet again, and repeat. If you time the maneuver so that the upward pull from the leash happens just before the push on his rump, you should be able to progress to the point where the slight upward pull will be the cue for the dog to sit. It shouldn't take long for the pup to pick up on this basic command.

Upward pressure on the neck with downward pressure on the rump is one way to teach "sit."

Hold your hand out like a traffic cop for "stay." Eventually increase the distance you move away and the length of time you require the dog to remain in that position.

Stay

"Stay" works best once "sit" has been mastered. Some people use "sit" to mean both "sit" and "stay"; I like the added word. To me, it reinforces what's wanted, and correcting the dog becomes easier should he sit properly but not stay. He'll know where the infraction occurred.

Starting from the sit position, simply move a few feet away while saying, "Stay," and holding your palm out like a traffic cop. Make sure you leave a few seconds of silence between the "sit" and "stay" commands so the dog can differentiate the actions

required of each. At first, don't expect the pup to last long; say a release command–such as "Okay!"–when it looks as if the dog is going to get up and move. Don't correct early on; keep the first few sessions fun, and time your release signal for when the dog is going to move. Clap your hands and whistle and move around a bit to encourage the dog to come back to you.

After several sessions, though, you can start to say "No" when the dog gets up. Take him by the leash back to the spot where he started, put him into a sit again, repeat the command and move away. This type of training–where you stop the dog for incorrect behavior and start again–is called *attrition*. There is still no discipline at this point; you are teaching. The pup will soon learn that to avoid being dragged back to the beginning, he needs to stay. Eventually, he'll remain in place, and you can increase the distance you move away and the length of time you require him to stay.

Keep a leash or a checkcord on the dog at all times so that should he break and run away, you won't have to chase him all over to get him back to the start. The checkcord will also help you guide him back toward you upon release, which will help greatly when it's time to teach the "come" command. In fact, you can even start saying this command as a release cue; coupled with the clapping and excited behavior, it will encourage movement in your direction.

You can begin to increase the distance you move away from the dog when he shows reliability at short distances over several sessions. As you start moving farther away, try walking around the dog in a circle, all the while saying, "Stay," and continuing to hold your hand out. Should he get up, put him back where he was sitting, give the "sit" command and start again.

Don't start disappearing the first time he holds a stay for over 5 seconds, but gradually increase the distance and the time. You should eventually progress to the point where you can go into another room or around the corner of the house, continuing to say, "Stay," every couple seconds, then release with an "Okay!" It will take many repetitions to get the dog to stay put, and you can expect a relapse in a reliable "stayer" when you start disappearing the first few times. Consistent, fair rewards and praise coupled with attrition are the best teachers.

Also consider that you don't have to walk away from the dog to get him to stay; he needs to learn that "stay" means to remain sitting in a variety of situations. So if you're walking with the dog on the leash, tell him to sit and stay while he's by your side. You may have to keep your hand on his rump to make sure he keeps it down. Pet and stroke his shoulders, and then release him when you start moving again.

Another good teacher is, once again, the dog's food bowl—with some dogs, the path to their brain passes through the stomach. If you've already got your dog sitting nicely for his dinner, set the dish down slowly as you say, "Stay," holding your hand out between him and the food dish. As soon as he starts to move toward it, pick it up, take the dog back to where he was sitting before and repeat. With any movement from the dog, the dish comes up. Sooner or later, you'll be able to set the dish down and he won't break—then just give him an "Okay!" and let him dig in. You can begin increasing the distance between him and the dish and the time he's required to wait. Just be ready with a paper towel to wipe up the drool.

Feeding time is a great opportunity to practice both "sit" and "stay." The dog is especially motivated when food is the focus and the reward.

Come

Retriever trainers Amy and John Dahl say, "Coming when called represents a higher level of responsibility than heeling while on a lead, or sitting for attention [or supper] inside the house. Instead of being near you, anticipating praise or a reward, your [dog] is involved in a distracting activity and probably not thinking about you. Your voice, made fainter by distance, does not intrude strongly on your [dog's] awareness. Dogs ordinarily respond to a combination of gesture and situation cues as well as verbal command; but when you call your [dog], that faint, distinct voice is the only stimulus. The 'come' command alone must get your [dog's] attention, overriding the appeal of whatever he or she is doing."

This is why the "come" command is one of the most important commands you can teach a dog—especially since that "distracting activity" could possibly lead to harm. If your dog will come reliably when called, under any situation, then you'll always have a measure of control over him that will give you some comfort. The fact that your voice becomes fainter over extended distances is the primary reason for using a whistle once the dog learns the command. (Whistle commands for "sit" and "come" will be covered later.)

It's generally beneficial to start a new lesson when a dog understands the previous lesson well. But you can start saying the "come" command while you're working on "stay"; there's no harm in beginning to tie the two together. You may want to use a hallway with all doors closed as a space for this early training, reducing the dog's escape options. With the dog in a "sit" and "stay" position—and on a checkcord—bend down and clap your hands while saying, "Come!" Then use the checkcord to guide the dog toward you. You don't want to reel the pup in like a fish; just guide him. If he veers off in another direction, hold firm until he hits the end of the checkcord. Then use those collar taps again—tug, release, tug, release—to get him started back toward you. Keep taking up the slack as he approaches so that his feet don't get tangled up. Always be enthusiastic and encouraging, and praise for good behavior. This is a good place to use treats as rewards from time to time, too.

That's really about all there is to it. Once you've started, teaching "come" is a matter of *constant repetition*. One important point is to not keep repeating the command if the dog does not obey. If you think the dog won't come when you call, then go get him. Those distracting activities that John and Amy Dahl spoke about can be very entertaining; the Dahls say, "The most important pitfalls to avoid are (1) calling your [dog] when you cannot enforce [the command] and (2) attaching unpleasant consequences to coming when called."

In other words, if the "come" command is always tied to a reprimand for getting into trouble, a ceasing of playtime, a quitting of training or hunting, or your displeasure, it's safe to assume a dog will

With "taps" from the leash, you can get your dog on his feet to come to you.

develop negative feelings toward that command. True, you will at times have to call your dog for these reasons, but you also need to keep this training fun by calling him to begin things or to receive praise, too.

You'll need to practice this command in lots of different settings amid lots of different distractions to get total reliability. Always keep that checkcord on the pup while he's learning the command; you can expect a little relapse when he's taken off the cord, as he'll realize you can't control him or enforce commands as easily. This is one of the reasons most people decide to use an electronic collar as a "long-distance checkcord." Positive reinforcement of the command will teach your pup that good things happen when he "comes," and that understanding will help him become reliable. Just keep practicing.

Heel

"Heel" is the next command in the evolution of a pup's obedience skills. This command is especially important for a retriever to perform expertly because almost all of a retriever's work begins at your side as you line him up for a fetch. Before starting work on this command, it's a good idea to make sure the dog understands "sit," "stay" and "come" reliably, because all three are used in teaching "heel."

To get started, pick the side you wish to have the dog heel on, and stick with that side. Most people have their dog heel on the side opposite where they carry their gun. For a right-hander, that means the dog would heel on the left.

It's best to work on the "heel" command with the dog on a leash and a collar positioned on the pressure points

Say "Heel" whenever the pup is in the proper position, and don't yank if he gets out of place. Let him "pop" himself and then guide him back into place.

above the ears as described earlier. This is a perfect time to use a training tool designed to fit on the pressure points, such as the Command Lead or EZ Lead. To prevent the dog from wandering off to the side, you can begin this command alongside a house or fence, with the dog in between. If the dog won't heel, he'll be able to go only forward or backward, both of which are easy to correct.

Start with the dog in a "sit" position, move to his side so you're both facing the same way and begin walking, encouraging the dog to go with you by slapping your leg and using collar taps. If he knows the "come" command, you can use it to get him on his feet at first. But eventually, you want the dog to learn that "heel" means he should come from wherever he is to a location by your side, either to stay still or to walk with you.

The dog's proper position for heeling is by your side—his neck should be in line with your knee, which will allow him to see the direction you move. As long as the dog maintains this position, repeat, "Heel." When he lags behind, say, "No, heel," and guide him back into position alongside

you. Do the same thing when he bolts forward—stop walking and hold tight. Don't yank him back but let him pop himself when he hits the end of the leash. Say, "No, heel," and guide him back into position, continuing to pat your leg. Praise and keep walking when he's in the right position.

Periodically stop walking. What should happen next depends on the type of dog you have. Traditionally, pointing dogs remain standing when they are brought to a halt while on heel; retrievers are to sit. Some pointing dog trainers stop their dogs while on heel with the "whoa" command, one they will use later in the field. Stand still for a few moments and begin walking again, saying, "Heel." With enough repetition, he will learn that when you stop, he is to also stop and sit or stand still.

Once he's walking well in a straight line, start putting in turns. Be ready for him to bump into your legs or get far out of position. Use the leash to keep him away from you when you turn toward him and to pull him closer when you turn away from him. If you've worked on keeping his neck at your knee, he'll see turns coming more easily and will adjust his pace to stay in the right area.

When the dog is proficient at all of these basic heeling situations, start mixing them up. One thing that tests a dog's understanding of the command—and really reinforces "sit" and "stay"—is to tell him to sit while you're still walking with him in the "heel" position. Before, he stopped only when you stopped; now he is to stop while you're still moving. It will be confusing at first, so stop with him as you say, "Sit." Gradually decrease the time you stay put before moving again. Say, "Stay," when you start to move to let the dog know he is to remain where he is.

Eventually, you should be able to halt the dog without breaking pace yourself; while walking the dog on "heel," you'll be able to say, "Sit, stay," and keep right on walking. Saying "Heel" again will bring the dog back up into position, where you can give him a good rub on the shoulders for being a good boy. Sitting and staying on heel have the most practical applicability with retrievers, but they're good tools for imprinting obedience with any kind of dog.

Occasionally give him a "sit" command and keep walking. Start to mingle his commands once he becomes proficient at them.

Down

If you have a retriever and plan to do a lot of waterfowl hunting in a field or a low-profile boat, this is a very valuable command. It allows you to get the dog hidden when needed, even covered up with a camouflage blanket or tarp. And it's one of the most sanity-preserving commands a family dog can learn. (It's particularly handy when you have non-dog-friendly guests who just don't appreciate your pup's foot-long string of drool hanging to the floor during dinnertime.)

I like to teach this command on the pad the dog sleeps on, or in a particular spot where I'd like him to stay calm and quiet in the house. To begin, the dog should be sitting. Slowly sweep out his front legs and gently push down, keeping hold of his collar, and say, "Down." Try not to grasp the dog's feet or toes, as most don't like this; rather, work higher up on his legs and pull them forward. You'll need to watch the dog's rump to make sure that he doesn't pop up when you start moving his legs forward. When he's down, tell

him to stay, pet him and then release. This is a good time to give a treat.

Once he's following the spoken command, squat in front of the sitting dog, say, "Down," as you lower your hand in front of his face, and move your whole body to the ground. This body language is clear to the dog. With practice, you should be able to get the attention of a sitting dog across the room—or out in the field—and silently lower your hand to the ground to get the dog to lie down.

Some people use the "down" command with dogs that like to jump up on people. In my opinion, this can lead to confusion because in one instance, you're happy if he lies on the floor; in the other, you're happy if the dog simply doesn't jump anymore. So I use "off" to tell a dog not to jump up on people. Try a gentle knee to the chest of the leaping dog; grab his front paws and throw them to the side while saying a stern, "Off!" As with teaching the dog not to play-bite, you can also use a hurt "Ow!" when he puts his paws on you; this might clue him in to the fact that he's being naughty.

A little language on your part can help in teaching "down." Eventually, you may be able to get your dog to do it on the hand gesture alone.

Kennel

As discussed in Chapter Three, you should work on this command right from day one, just like "Outside!" for housebreaking. If you've done so, your pup has always been put inside his crate whenever you left or traveled anywhere. And every time you put him in, you said his command to kennel.

During the pup's formal obedience training, it's a good idea to reinforce these early lessons with more structured training. Make sure to move the crate around, and work on this command wherever you plan to use it—particularly in the bed of a truck or an SUV.

Start off fun by placing the dog in a "sit" and "stay" in front of his open crate, tossing a treat in and saying, "Kennel!" to get him inside. Close and latch the gate behind him. Just as when he was really young, let him out only if he's quiet (which he should be now that he's older and understands that's the only way to get out).

To formally teach the command, run the checkcord from his collar through the front of the kennel and out the back (or out the side window and then to the back). Put the dog in a "sit" and "stay" in front of his open crate, take up the checkcord behind the kennel and say, "Kennel!" as you give taps with the checkcord.

Since by now the pup knows how to respond to those taps on his collar, he'll get up and start toward you—and at first he'll avoid the crate. When he does, say, "No," take him back to the start and repeat. He'll soon walk right into the crate. When he does, tell him to sit, walk to the front and close the door. After that, it's a matter of repetition.

Whistle Commands

Whistle commands, which are taught after a hunting dog thoroughly understands verbal commands, are vital for communicating with him at a distance. Wind, waves, rustling brush and sheer distance will whisk away your voice in the field, but a high-pitched whistle will cut through these noises easily. Some dogs seem to respond better to a whistle, too, because it is consistent and has none of the emotion that may affect how the dog interprets a verbal command. A stern "Sit!" versus a pleading "Sit?" can be confusing—your tone, inflection and even pronunciation may be different. Sure, the dog should respond no matter what, but the fact is that most won't. With practice, though, a sharp whistle blast will sound the same time after time—and will generate the same response.

"Sit" and "come" are the two main commands that have a corresponding whistle. With retrievers, use both extensively; with pointing dogs you may use

One way to formally teach the "kennel" command is to use the dog's understanding of what the "taps" on his leash mean. Be ready for him to avoid the crate at first!

Whistle commands for "sit" and "come" are some of the most important you can teach your dog. The whistle will carry over the wind and distance when your voice will not.

only the "come" whistle. The type of whistle doesn't matter as much as how you blow it—you want sharp, almost ear-piercing blasts for "sit" and a trilling toot-toot-toot for "come."

Sit. There are three ways to get a dog to sit: the pull-up-push-down maneuver, the spoken command and the whistle blast. Your dog already knows two of these, and once this is accomplished, it is very easy to teach the third. To teach "sit" with a whistle, put the leash and collar on the dog and use the pull-up-push-down maneuver, saying, "Sit!" as you push his rump down. Because the dog is practiced at this, you'll probably find that the initial upward tap on the collar will prompt the sit. That's great.

Now substitute one whistle blast for the spoken command just as you begin to push his rump down. This was the way you taught him to respond to the spoken command, using the physical manipulation as a precursor to the spoken cue; the whistle now becomes the cue you want the dog to respond to. Once you've done this for several repetitions, start using the spoken command as the precursor to the whistle cue: "Sit!" Toot! Begin to phase out the spoken command every third or fourth time, and before you know it, the dog will sit with one whistle blast.

Start extending the distance between you and the dog to begin development of a long-distance sit. If he starts to move toward you when you blow the whistle, take quick steps toward him, holding your hand up like a traffic cop to stop him, and whistle once again, saying, "Sit!" If you have a checkcord on the dog, you can flip a loop into it that will run the length of the cord and tap upward on his collar—another reminder that he is to sit.

Come. Just as there are three ways to get a dog to sit, there are three ways to get him to come. String them together in the same manner. With the dog on a "sit" and "stay," move away from him, tug-release on his collar with the checkcord and say, "Come!" This serves as a refresher for the dog. After several repetitions, begin to use your trilling toot-toot-toot just as you tug on the cord to get him to come. You might find that the dog loves the whistle and will come much more enthusiastically to it than to your spoken command. The whistle sounds more exciting, I think, especially if you clap your hands, too. Then begin to just say, "Come!" and trill on the whistle to link the spoken and whistle commands. Finally, phase out the spoken command until the dog responds to the whistle alone.

Putting It All Together

It may seem to take forever to teach these simple obedience commands, and for some, it will take forever! Some dogs pick up commands faster than others, but a dog that takes a long time isn't a dud. All dogs learn at a different pace; you should progress at your dog's own speed.

But once those commands are learned, all is not done. In fact, this type of training should not be finished at all—not throughout a dog's entire life. Do some exercises and repetitions of these commands in a training situation every day. The best way to get through a lot of them in a hurry is to put them all together.

The following sequence works wonderfully with retrievers in developing the proper delivery of a bird to hand. With pointing dogs, this exercise is extremely useful when you're hunting near roads or vehicles, provided you can trust the dog to obey.

Start by heeling the dog on a straight walk, add in a couple turns and tell the dog to sit and stay, either verbally or with a whistle. (If you're working with a pointing dog, have him stop in some manner). Keep walking a short distance away, turn and face the dog and command him to come. As the dog approaches you, command, "Heel," and guide him into position near your side, helping him turn so that he's facing the same direction you are. If you have a retriever, direct him to sit again; a

pointing dog should stop. Give a good rub on the shoulders with some verbal praise and keep repeating. This is the position a retriever will be in when he brings back a bird or a bumper, so you might want to work more extensively on this sequence to get it down perfectly.

Next, start extending the distances. Increase the time that the dog is required to heel or stay. As he's coming to you, give him an extra whistle-sit command. Always bring him to the finishing position near your side, guiding him with the checkcord if he starts to wander or run past you, and helping him turn to face the same direction you are. After he performs the sequence correctly, give him a few seconds, then praise him for a job well done.

After this, repeat in lots of environments amid lots of distractions (other people, other animals, interesting objects scattered about to play with or inspect, etc.) to get reliability. Learn to recognize those times when the dog just wants to goof off, and have fun goofing off with him. Enjoy him while he's still a puppy.

As I mentioned earlier, keep in mind that it's a mistake to try to make a dog fit into a specific training regimen—you need to modify the regimen to fit the dog. Short sessions will keep a dog's attention longer, and it won't be like pulling teeth to get him to obey. If you find yourself saying, "Just one more time, and we'll quit," quit. You're only asking for trouble by pushing.

Recognize when your pup's attention span is waning—and goof off with him. Never forget to let your dog be a dog!

Introduction to Birds

A nice break from obedience training—which can become pretty monotonous for both the trainer and the dog—is to introduce some birds. This activity should always be supervised, of course, and you'll want to start off with dead birds at first. Frozen pigeons or quail or chukars make a nice introduction because a dog can get his mouth around them.

If your pup is still young, hold him in your arms and bring out the bird. Let him sniff and snarf and mouth and tug and pull and play with the bird. Talk nicely to him, telling him what a wonderful dog he is. Let the feathers tickle his nose. Don't ever punish or correct the dog at this point—grin and bear it if the pup nails your fingers unknowingly while biting down on the bird. Keep the atmosphere fun. Have a partner fire a blank pistol from 50 yards or so away so that the dog starts to associate gunfire with birds.

As the dog starts to mature and you begin working on obedience, continue to expose him to birds every so often. Start bringing in freshly shot birds so that he can feel the warm feathers and body, and don't expect too much out of him. If you have a pointing dog, don't expect him to lock up solidly—let him react however he wants. We'll start expecting better manners when he's a touch older. If you have a retriever, toss the bird a short distance for him and let him tackle it and pick it up. If the dog picks up a bird, try to coax him back to you.

If you want to introduce live birds, stick with chukars, quail or pigeons. Pheasants and ducks are way too big for a young dog, and they can easily stand their ground and fight. You don't ever want to scare a pup in his first experiences with birds. You'll use real birds in formal hunting training, but right now, the main goal is to get the pup used to feathers—and to really get his juices flowing for birds.

TEN COMMANDMENTS OF BASIC TRAINING

This chapter began with the observation that basic obedience training is the most valuable training we can give the family/hunting dog; basic commands will become the foundation of the more advanced skills he'll use for hunting. To recap the tips we've covered, here are my Ten Commandments of Basic Training to keep in mind while teaching and maintaining obedience skills.

1. Don't tie your training to timetables. Proceed at your dog's pace. Move on to the next command only when he thoroughly understands the current lesson. Not only are breeds of dogs different in their learning abilities, but dogs within the same breed are also unique. What one may pick up in two sessions at 10 weeks of age may take a 14-week-old a month to learn.

2. When you feel yourself getting frustrated or angry, quit. The potential rewards of getting your dog to comply when you're operating with a short fuse are not worth the risks.

3. Several short lessons of 5- to 15-minute duration are better than a few long, drawn-out exercises. Shorter sessions are easier to work into your schedule, and you have a better chance of keeping up the dog's spirits and enthusiasm. When the pup's attention begins to wander, it's time to quit—and it's an indication that you went too long; the next session should be shorter. Also, any kind of training in hot weather should be kept very short.

4. Don't give a command unless you can enforce it or physically manipulate the dog into complying, such as by guiding him into a "heel" position or pushing his rump down to sit.

5. Before administering any discipline or correction, make absolutely sure that the dog truly understands what's being asked. Discipline should be saved for outright defiance, not incorrect attempts to do what you're asking.

6. Repetition, repetition, repetition is the key to teaching basic obedience commands.

7. Train in different locations amid distractions after the dog has learned a command to get reliable obedience.

8. Simplify your lessons and praise every improvement. If your dog is having trouble with a new lesson, simplify what you're asking him to do until he understands. Build in a stepwise fashion from that point, praising every step forward.

9. Make sure that others who give the dog basic obedience commands say the commands, enforce them and praise the dog in a consistent manner. The dog should be expected to perform each command the same way, no matter who gives it.

10. Always end on a positive note. Even if that means nothing more than a simple "sit," finish with something you know the dog can do. Verbally praise, rub his shoulders and let him go play.

CHAPTER SIX

Training Exercises for the Hunting Retriever

A retriever is not just going to sit, stay, come and heel throughout his hunting career. He'll have to execute retrieves in some pretty demanding situations, and he'll need a skill set that will carry him successfully toward his goal. Now is when the fun begins—training your retriever to perform these advanced skills to make him reliable, keep him out of danger and recover that bird.

If possible, you'll want to have help with some of these drills. If you can find a hunting partner who's also starting out with a young dog, this is an excellent time to help each other out—and teach both dogs self-control by having them watch each other make retrieves. But you will want to do the introduction to these drills alone; help is usually needed only when you start increasing the distance on fetches.

In many ways, the Ten Commandments of Basic Training apply to more advanced training as well. Remember to build up to complicated skills in your training sessions, and don't introduce an entirely new concept and all its facets at once. For example, don't start off teaching all the hand signals in the very first session; stick with one for as long as it takes the dog to master it, then introduce another. Don't require your dog to master taking long straight lines to marks and blinds if it's the first time he's done either one. Introduce new

concepts in steps; take the drills from this or other books and videos and break them down into their component parts. Training in this fashion will lead to a happier dog that is successful early on.

As with basic obedience training, always end your training sessions on a positive note, even if it's with a short fetch or some work on "sit" and "stay" and "heel." In fact, that's a great way to begin and end each training session, with a calm run-through of obedience commands. It can really settle down a hyperactive dog that's just itching to get into the water for some fetches.

I'm not going to present a timetable for these drills, except for the force-fetch exercise, which is based on a dog's physical development, not his mental development. Every dog is different and progresses at different rates. (You may also find that some skills are more easily taught after a dog has a hunting season or two under his belt.) Don't be discouraged if your dog takes longer than your buddy's—this isn't a contest. You want the most reliable, efficient hunting dog you can get, and sometimes that takes time; or you may have a pup that just cruises through the training. Take it easy, don't expect too much of the pup, don't push him on to the next step too soon, and have fun. It takes as long as it takes. Again, if you find yourself getting frustrated, quit.

Black Labs and pheasants are a match made in many hunter's dreams.

The skills you require of your retriever will depend largely on the type of hunting you like to do.

Skills for the Hunting Retriever

People teach retrievers many, many drills, some pretty complicated. As a hunter, you may never use many of the really advanced setups and skills, such as those carried out to extreme distances. If you compete with your dog, he'll need to become an expert at these demanding exercises, which may require the services of a professional trainer. But what you ask your dog to do over the course of his life as a hunter might be surprising—both in its simplicity and in the difficult situations that occasionally arise.

It all depends on how, where and what you hunt. When I lived in South Dakota, duck hunting took place on the edge of potholes, small ponds in the middle of vast farm country. We didn't use boats. Josie was educated very quickly—plenty of ducks, plenty of shooting and great conditions for a puppy to mark birds and get lots of experience. Had Josie lived her entire life in South Dakota, the skills she would've needed were handling, retrieves (both marks and blinds) up to a couple hundred yards, upland hunting skills, how to search for dead birds, and blind manners such as letting another dog get a fetch, staying quiet and still, etc. That's about it, besides basic obedience, of course. If she couldn't perform some of the more exacting skills (taking a long straight line, not cheating along the bank, not popping, etc.), it didn't really matter because I could always walk out with her or redirect her to help achieve our primary goal—collecting the bird.

But now that we live in Michigan, Josie needs to learn a whole new set of skills, and I need to greatly reinforce some that she was allowed to slack off on in South Dakota. Now we hunt out of a boat, so there is a greater demand for obedience; the waters are deeper and more treacherous, requiring her to take very straight lines so that she gets in and out quickly. Some of the distances are much greater, and I can't go out there and help her like I could in South Dakota. There are more fur trappers around, so I don't want her to run along the bank in marshes for fear of her stumbling into a trap. Our upland hunting was once mostly for pheasant in open grass; now we hunt different upland birds in thicker cover, requiring her to modify the range at which she hunts. In many cases, I've had to teach a new command or go back to the drawing board to either teach new skills or reinforce old ones.

We all like to see our dogs perform flawlessly, and during your hunts, you'll see areas that will need more work. That's why you should keep a detailed journal of the types of retrieves and conditions your dog hunts in—it will give you an idea of where work is needed during the training season. One season in South Dakota, over 80 percent of my Lab's retrieves were *decoy marks* (ducks that fell dead in the decoys), presenting easy fetches of less than 40 yards. Only one or two were *sailers* over 150 yards (crippled birds, especially geese, that can sail, or glide, quite a distance).

Did these facts prompt me to totally ignore long-distance retrieves during our training? No; we worked on various distances. When I needed her to execute a demanding retrieve, it certainly was nice that she had that skill. But in our training, I emphasized the types of retrieves she did the most so that she could perform them expertly.

So be sure to analyze the kind of hunting you do as you decide how to train your retriever. Jump-shooting may require more obedience than sitting in a blind all day; hunting the ocean coastline may require different advanced skills than hunting in potholes. Also keep a log of the types of retrieves and conditions your dog encounters during the year. That information will point to the strengths and weaknesses in your training program. The skills presented in this chapter are common enough to cover just about every hunting situation—they're skills that every hunting retriever should know—and they're advanced enough to prepare your dog for those few arduous retrieves he'll more than likely encounter each year.

Getting the Pup Started with Play Retrieves

Nothing is more exciting than seeing those first few glimpses of a dog's potential, and those puppy play retrieves are a great way to begin building his enthusiasm. Bloodlines and pedigrees will be the biggest determining factor in a dog's inherent drive to pick things up, but if you're excited and positive when your pup begins bringing things back to you, he'll see how much fun it really is.

A rolled-up sock works great because a pup can easily pick it up. Start on your hands and knees in a closed-off hallway, where there is no place for the dog to go except back to you. Tease the dog with the sock, snatching it from under his paws as he tries to pounce, and then toss it. He will naturally go get it.

He'll likely come charging back, trying to get past you. Catch him as if he were coming to you, praise him and toss the sock again. If he doesn't come, start clapping and whistling and moving backward, around the corner and out of sight if need be. He'll grow curious and come—sometimes with the sock, sometimes without. Scoop him up and praise him, letting him continue to hold the sock. Then gently open his mouth as you say the release command, "Give," take the sock out and toss it for him again. Let him chase and have fun. You can't expect the dog to learn or know what the "give" command means at this point, but saying it whenever you gently take something out of his mouth lays a foundation for later lessons.

You can start using a canvas puppy bumper when he's a little older, and start moving the game—which is what it should be at this point—to different places. I like using our raised deck; it's a little more open than a hallway, but there's still only one place to go. You'll be amazed at how quickly the pup will learn that if he comes back to you with the object, the game continues.

Nothing is more exciting than seeing those first puppy fetches.

Steadiness

As your dog starts to figure this game out, you can begin to lay the groundwork for his future steadiness by restraining him for a few moments before letting him fetch. As you let him go, say his name—which will be his release command to fetch objects he can see—and let him tackle the object. Hold him in your hands a little longer each time, and occasionally let go to see if he'll stay on his own. With lots of repetitions, he'll begin to naturally develop the skill of waiting until he hears his name before dashing from your side.

You can continue play-retrieving all through obedience training and even begin to incorporate obedience commands. Put a checkcord on the dog and give him a "sit" command followed by a "stay" command. Toss the bumper a short distance, keeping him steady at your side with the checkcord,

Once your pup has great enthusiasm, it doesn't hurt to start holding him back to encourage steadiness.

and release him. Now that you're no longer in a hallway or on the deck, you'll have to guide him back to you after he makes the fetch.

Always stress steadiness—a dog that breaks when he sees ducks coming in or hears a shot is a safety hazard, especially if you're hunting out of a boat. The earlier you can lay a foundation for steady behavior, the better; this means keeping a cord on the dog for a long time. As he becomes more reliable with the "come" command, you can shorten the cord; you may eventually only need to grasp him by the collar, and hopefully you'll get beyond that, too.

Additional Commands for the Hunting Retriever

In addition to the basic obedience commands that provide a foundation for all of a dog's training and control in the field, you may find some of the following commands useful for specialized situations.

Dead Bird. For upland hunters—or for those who hunt waterfowl in places where the bird may fall in thick cover—this is an extremely useful command. It tells the dog that he's in the vicinity where you last saw the bird, and it cues him to get his nose on the ground and search methodically to find it. If you say the command in a low, purring voice—*"Deeeaaaddd biiirrrrddd"*—while moving your hand over the area of the fall, it really gets the dog excited.

One way to start training this command is by hiding little pieces of hot dog in the yard. Scatter them about and walk around with your dog, cooing, *"Deeaadd biirrdd"* while motioning in the vicinity of a slice. Once the dog learns that there's something good—a piece of food, a bumper or a bird—on the ground when you say that command, he'll stick his schnoz on the ground and sniff enthusiastically until he finds it. Don't worry that when you move to birds he'll try to eat those, too. It doesn't happen.

Start saying this command whenever the dog approaches his bumpers on a fetch—even if they're marked retrieves that he can see the entire time he runs out to them. Continue to say it once the bumpers are thrown into deeper cover. Next smear bottled scent on some canvas bumpers, trail a path through high weeds without the dog seeing, bring him in and start repeating, "Dead bird," while motioning to the area where the track starts. Keep repeating the command as he searches with his nose on the ground; if he wanders off course, call him back and say, "Dead bird," again. Occasionally use some recently shot or frozen birds to really get the dog going.

Here. A lot of people use the "here" command in place of "come," but I use it to mean "pay attention to me because I'm going to give you a direction." I use it when I handle or line up the dog; it prevents him from swinging his head or not looking where I'm pointing. When a dog is out at a distance and I stop him with the whistle, I use "here" to get him to snap his eyes onto me in anticipation of a command to come or a direction to cast. When he's at my side, the "here" command gets him to peer down the line I indicate instead of looking all around. It zeroes him in to the fact that at any second, he's going to get to fetch. In a sense, it is a one-word way to say, "I want you to go 'here' in order to find the bumper or bird."

This command really prompts the dog to look at your hand, for that is what indicates the direction. Start teaching this command with the dog at your side as you line him up for a retrieve. With the dog at "heel," toss a bumper a short distance.

Pointing your hand at the bumper, place your hand off the end of his nose, just above it. Then say, "Here," while snapping the fingers of your lining hand to get him to look at the bumper. As soon as he is gazing in the proper direction, release him on his name. Sometimes he won't look down your hand; simply repeat the "here" command and snap again. Don't release him until he looks down your hand and holds the stare for a second or two.

As soon as the dog begins to take cues from your hand, toss two bumpers out at a wide angle apart. Now you'll teach him to look from one bumper to the next by the way you line him. With the leash on, properly align him to one bumper, position your hand with an accompanying "here" command, and then pivot to the other bumper. (The leash will help to pull him off the first bumper.) Snap your fingers and line your hand toward the other bumper, commanding "Here" again. Switching between bumpers helps develop in the dog a good habit of marking downed bumpers and can help him commit their locations to memory. Once the dog is looking down your hand, release him, bring him back to "heel," take the bumper, line him up on the other bumper and send him. Be aware that a young pup will often go for the last bumper thrown regardless of where you send him. Don't be discouraged; all pups do this, and with training, they all learn to go to the one they're sent for.

The "dead bird" command will tell the dog to get his nose in the ground to search for a downed bird.

This training conveys to the dog the fact that you will always give him the proper direction toward a fetch, and it helps develop trust between you. It's vital that your dog never think that you're going to send him someplace where there won't be anything to retrieve, especially early on.

Leave It. This is a very useful command for preventing your retriever from picking up something or making him drop something he shouldn't have. You'll use it a lot around your home. It's different than the "give" command, where you accept something from the dog. "Leave it" makes the dog drop an object and ignore it.

As you work with the dog in developing the "fetch," "hold" and "give" commands, you can start to implement "leave it" when the dog attempts to pick up things that you didn't indicate. Start by telling the dog, "No, leave it," removing the object (which is usually trash or laundry or some other item you don't want him to have) and putting it back in its original location. If the dog attempts to pick it up again, repeat, "No, leave it." After many repetitions, the dog will learn to resist

"Leave it" is a useful command in both the field and at home.

the urge to fetch at this command and instead find something else.

In hunting, I have used this command to get a dog to drop a dead duck in the water and instead retrieve another dead bird that may be drifting into a difficult location. Or sometimes a dog may get into something dangerous, and you may not be in a position to go corral him away from the hazard. Being able to command "Leave it!" will do the job.

Quiet. Nothing is more aggravating—or harder to cure—than a retriever that constantly whines in the duck blind. While a bark collar may appear to be the answer, a dog will usually find the noise level that is just quiet enough to not produce a correction from the collar. A firm "No!" doesn't seem to work either, as the dog just can't seem to get a handle on his enthusiasm and lets it escape in a pleading whimper.

Start off when the dog is a pup by giving the "quiet" command whenever he's howling. If he hears it enough, he might put together that the command and the subsequent praise for silent behavior are good things.

The method that has perhaps proven the most useful in curing this annoying behavior will require loads of time and patience on your part—denying any sort of a retrieve to a dog that vocalizes while he's waiting by your side. When you toss a bumper to be fetched, if the dog whines or barks or makes any other sort of noise, put the dog on a firm "stay" and go out and pick up the bumper yourself. Or have a training partner get it—every single time. You cannot deviate and let him have a fetch some of the time. Every time he whines, he must be denied the retrieve.

You might think that you can use this method during the training season, but the hunting season is a different matter. You've worked so hard to get to the point where you can go hunting with your dog that you want him to have as many retrieves as possible. But whining pops up with greater force while hunting, and if this behavior really bothers you, you'll have to be vigilant even during the hunting season and retrieve the birds yourself. If you can train by shooting live birds in the off-season, that's a big bonus and you might solve the problem. But if the dog only sees birds shot during the hunting season, it will be extremely difficult for him to control his excitement.

In truth, this trait is only rarely correctable. It seems to be less a matter of what the dog does than what the dog is. If you have a vocalizing dog, you are likely stuck with him. I'd suggest you get a bark collar and learn to live with the soft background noise. Think of it as your dog's theme song.

Spot. This command instructs a dog to seek out and stay in a certain spot until given a release command. It builds upon the "stay" command to correspond with a certain place—a tree stand, a piece of carpeting, a platform, a dog pad, etc.—that the dog can find and stay put on. It is very useful at home, particularly when guests come to visit, as the dog won't mob them at the door. It also helps to reinforce the "stay" command when you're hunting out of a boat by giving the dog his own hunting spot from which to wait.

Starting in your home, show the dog where his spot is—a rug by the back door, his dog pad, etc.—by leading him there on a leash while saying, "Spot!" Once he gets on his spot, tell him to sit and stay, then walk away. Give it a few seconds and then call him to you with "Okay!" or "Come!" to let him know he's off the hook.

Take him back to where you started before, about 10 or 15 feet away from the designated place, pause, and then repeat, "Spot!" as you begin walking toward the rug or pad. Keep saying it as you're walking, and once he sets foot on his place, put him into a "sit" and "stay" and then wait again. I like to say the word and pet the dog while he's on his spot to let him know that good things happen in this place.

After many repetitions starting from various points, you'll find that you won't need to walk him all the way to his spot—once he sees his spot, it will click that this particular rug or pad is his destination, and he'll hustle there to sit on his own. If you treat the dog upon successful completion, he'll really start hustling!

In the beginning, it's best to stick with only one spot so that it becomes familiar. Continue to practice and train from all points in your home until the dog can find his spot on his own upon hearing the command.

When the dog is reliable inside, begin identifying other places where he is to sit. Maybe it's a particular area in the bow of the boat or a dog platform that he'll sit on while hunting, attached to a tree or the edge of the boat. Identify these new spots the same way you did when teaching the command initially; this stage will be quicker because the dog is familiar with what he needs to do in response to that command—he just needs to learn where to do it.

To reinforce the command, using the food dish really helps; it speaks right to a dog's soul. When giving the command at mealtime, you'll find that you only need to whisper it and he'll zoom to his spot, leaving skid marks. Put him on his spot while you're holding his food dish and begin to set it down. Any time he makes a movement, stand back up. Keep standing up and refusing to give him his dinner until he can stay sitting on his spot until you release him.

The "spot" command will identify a particular place for the dog to stay in while hunting or around the home.

When teaching the remote sit, start close to the dog and increase the distance slowly. It's one of the most valuable skills for a hunting retriever to have.

The Remote Sit

Building on the whistle sit we looked at in the previous chapter is the remote sit, the skill of getting a retriever to sit at a distance when he hears a single whistle blast. The remote sit is one of the most fundamental–and essential–skills a retriever must know. All attempts at handling, keeping a dog out of danger, steering him back on line and communicating with him when he's out in the field and away from your side stem from his ability to sit his rump down and look at you.

The remote sit isn't difficult to teach, provided the dog is very reliable at the whistle sit. The whistle will be necessary because your voice may not carry well through cover or wind or choppy water; a sharp whistle blast will. So practice the whistle sit repeatedly with the dog in the yard, in the "heel" position, before giving him his dinner, on walks and anywhere you might say the "sit" command; use the whistle as often as you can.

When you have confidence that the dog is a reliable whistle sitter, you're ready to move on to the remote sit. Start with the dog romping in the yard with his checkcord attached. Getting the dog to sit at the whistle blast is only half the battle–he also needs to look at you. So when you begin to teach this skill, first tell the dog to come to get him moving toward you; then blow the whistle-sit blast. That will get his focus on you from the start.

Follow the whistle immediately with a spoken "Sit!" Retriever trainer James Keldsen says, "Some dogs, rather than sit away from the trainer, will want to return to you and then sit–this is where pulling up on the lead will help. Flip the lead up so that the dog feels the lead pull up on its neck. Practice will get the technique down. You may even have to take a step toward the dog with your hand extended like a traffic cop, repeating a spoken 'sit' command and a single whistle blast." When you flip the checkcord, a loop will travel the length of the cord and gently jerk upward on the dog's collar, reminding him how he was initially taught to sit with the pull-up-push-down maneuver.

Continually practice this command until the dog obeys without question.

You can also start with the dog at your side. "When he leaves your side," Keldsen explains, "and is a little way out but not on a full run, command, 'Sit,' blow the whistle, and stop the dog with the [checkcord]. Wear a pair of gloves to prevent the rope from burning your hands. When the dog stops [he'll probably be standing], repeat the whistle blast; if necessary, walk to him and physically sit the dog. After he has sat for a few seconds, give him the break command [such as 'okay']." If the dog stops facing away from you, go to him and turn him around with the checkcord until he is facing where you were, walk back to your original location, wait a few seconds and release him. You may have to do this a few times, but stopping him with the cord will generally turn him around to face you as well.

After that, as with all training skills, the keys are repetition and maintaining a high expectation that every time you blow a single whistle blast while the dog is not at your side, he'll sit. If you think he's having a "moment" when your command will fall on deaf ears, don't give it unless you can enforce his compliance. Begin at short distances, and make a commotion about getting his rump down if he tries to scoot toward you.

Keldsen offers a final piece of advice: "Periodically, take the dog to the park or a friend's house and repeat the training sessions there. He needs to learn that he has to pay attention no matter where he is or what is going on around him. The more often and the more places this is done, the more reliable the dog will be in the end." The true test will come when you toss a bumper, release him for the fetch and then blow the whistle to stop him in his tracks. Don't do this unless you're sure that you can get him to comply—another reason to have the checkcord still attached to his collar.

With the dog on a run for a fetch, blow the whistle or command "sit" and hold tight to the checkcord.

Marked Retrieves

Those puppy retrieves you've been doing all this time are called *marks*–retrieves in which the dog sees the object fall to the ground, thereby "marking" its location. While you've been playing, you've been teaching the pup to follow the flight path of an object and then to run after it and fetch it. When the pup is getting better at obedience but still needs the checkcord attached, it's time to start formally teaching the proper technique for a mature marked retrieve.

Retriever trainer Evan Graham of Liberty, Missouri, says to start simple. "No cover or other factors that would impede success. When introducing a dog to anything that is new to him [or her], the most success-promoting approach is to keep it simple. Break any new function down into its most basic form."

The nicely mowed yard where you've been doing obedience training is a good place to start. Another good place is on a narrow walkway or a dirt trail that can help to influence the pup to take a straight line to the bumper right from the beginning.

It's a good idea to get into the habit of lining your dog to a retrieve, even when he sees an object fall and can see it lying there on the ground. The earlier your dog can trust your direction, the better off he'll be when it comes to running *blind* retrieves, where he doesn't see the fall of the bumper nor its placement on the ground–it is "blind" to him. Then he'll have to trust you to point him in the right direction, and he'll have to have the confidence to stay on that line until he finds the bumper with his eyes or nose. That's why starting off on a trail lets the dog easily identify it as a good idea right from the start. The dog will see the path to the bumper, and he'll learn to run straight to it.

Start by holding the dog's checkcord while he's sitting in the "heel" position, and toss the bumper down the path (about 20 yards or so) so that it lands in the center. The dog should be very alert to the bumper and itching to go; restrain him with the checkcord until he settles down, reminding him, "Stay." He should be pointed toward the bumper. Professional retriever trainer Butch Goodwin of Northern Flight Retrievers in New Plymouth, Idaho, says it will be evident he's ready to go "when his body is pointed in the correct direction, his ears go up, his body tenses and his gaze is fixed in an intense stare at a distant point."

Now line the dog using the hand on the side the dog is heeling–if he's on your left side, use your left hand; switch the cord to your right hand to keep him in place. "Once his attention is fixed and he is intensely focused in the direction you want him to go," Goodwin continues, "put your hand well out in front of his head and in a straight line between his eyes where he can look right past it at the line he will be running. Do not move your hand left or right once you put it down in position. If you need to change his line, take your hand away and realign his body, not just his head.

"Once you are satisfied with his body alignment, his gaze is fixed and your hand is in the correct position," says Goodwin, "give yourself a silent count of three, and send him. Do not hesitate or make him wait a long time once he has the 'picture' in his head or he will lose his focus. Do not use a 'bowler's sweep' of your hand and arm when you send him. Keep your hand perfectly still and don't move it until the dog has run and his tail has passed your hand."

Guide him back with the checkcord, and don't expect a perfect delivery at this point–that will come later, after you force-fetch the dog. But you should put the obedience commands together as you did earlier, bringing him back with a "come" command, guiding him into the "heel" position with the cord and a spoken command, and then finishing with a "sit" command. The sooner the dog can get into the habit of doing the same exact thing on the return of every retrieve, the faster the pattern will become second nature. Even if he drops the bumper at this point, let him drop it–or reach out and grab it before he drops it, encouraging him to take a couple

With marked retrieves, use bright white bumpers so the dog can see them clearly.

more steps toward you by backing up, then quickly reaching forward, saying, "Give" as you take the bumper. Then finish his position at your side.

By doing these early marked retrieves on a line that is clearly identifiable to the dog and to you, you're helping develop a dog that can carry himself in a straight line; and by placing your hand in front of the dog and indicating the line he is to take down this clear path, you're helping develop his trust in your direction. After all, he can see the bumper out there; he knows where it is. And you're pointing him in the right direction. As Evan Graham says, keep it simple and get rid of anything that might make the dog fail.

Moving off the path and into the neatly mowed grass, you'll need to be more conscious that you're sending the dog on the proper line. Graham suggests a little trick to keep that proper line in sight; it really helps once you move out to extreme distances. "The first thing to do is to find a landmark…one that you can find easily on or near the horizon that is in line with the fall. That will make it easier to keep your bearings.

"Then use that landmark to determine the true line," Graham continues. "Look to your landmark. Then lower your gaze across the spot of the fall, and continue lowering it right down your intended line to a spot roughly 3 feet in front of your dog. A leaf, a particular blade of grass, or even a split between blades of grass can identify this [spot]. The idea is that, once you have identified that spot close to your dog, you no longer need to look back and forth from the dog to the fall to determine if he is lined up right. If he's lined up for that spot, he's lined up for the fall."

Hunting in the field, you'll probably do more marked retrieves, with the dog starting out at your side, than anything

Always line your dog properly and be careful not to do a "bowler's sweep" once you release him.

Using a helper will allow you to increase the distance of retrieves and will get the dog looking "out there" for the marks.

else. So training throws shouldn't always come from you—when you're hunting, the birds won't come from your side; they'll be out there. This is where you need to employ the help of some "throwers" to go out into the field and throw bumpers for your dog. "Instruct your throwers to make their throws long and flat, far away from them and kept low so the bird or bumper remains easily in the pup's view throughout the entire fall," Graham recommends. "This should also keep the pup from being enticed to run to the [thrower] instead of the fall." As will the checkcord that he's still wearing.

Once again, it's about repetition, increasing distances, and perhaps some cover changes and new locations to keep the experience fresh and exciting for the dog. Distances should not exceed about 40 yards for much of the pup's first season of training; when obedience commands, marked and blind retrieves, handling skills and obedience to the whistle have been mastered, then you can move out to 100 yards or beyond.

Graham also suggests what he calls "walking singles" as a way to keep training new and exciting for the dog. "Each fall is a new fall, but still designed for success. Instruct your thrower to walk

a predetermined course by waiting until your pup is well on the way back with each mark, and then moving to where he will throw the next one. This is a great way to increase distance, as well, by having the thrower walk a course that gradually provides slightly longer marks each time."

Double Retrieves

To this point, the dog has made only single retrieves—one bumper thrown, one fetch made. When he's proficient at this, it's time to start introducing another bumper into the mix. Start off at the distance you initially started your single marks—within 20 yards—on clean ground. Throw one bumper and then, at a very wide angle, throw the other—both should be very visible, white bumpers on green grass. The dog will probably be very eager to fetch the last one he saw; line him up as you've been doing all along and send him for it. When he returns, take the bumper, and then line him up at the other bumper, which was the first one thrown; he should easily spot it on the ground and tear off after it once you release him at his name. Work on these easy doubles, mixed in with regular singles, for quite a while, even having your thrower toss

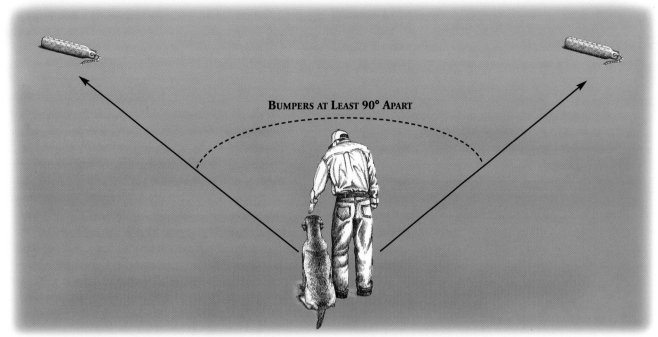

A basic double-marked retrieve setup: Throw each dummy about 20 yards away and at a wide angle (at least 90° apart).

some double retrieves. Don't be in too big a rush to start throwing multiple retrieves; you'll first need to read your dog to see when he's ready.

Stay vigilant in giving your dog straight, true lines; keep the bumpers highly visible and in low cover to promote success, and don't forget to praise your dog for a job well done. As soon as he starts to lose interest—you'll notice he won't look eagerly at the bumper while he's at heel, or he'll start to wander and get distracted by little things on his way to retrieve—go out and pick up the bumper, do a couple of obedience commands to end on a positive note, and put him up for the day.

Decoys and Gunfire

Don't forget to work your dog through some duck or goose decoys in these first marks. Lay a dozen or so out in the yard and walk your dog on the leash through them, letting him sniff them out and inspect them—but don't let him start chewing or attempt to pick them up. If he

Don't forget about decoys! Get your dog used to them by letting him do some fetches on the lawn.

does, simply say, "No!" or "Leave it!" as you take the decoy away and replace it. Once he seems to pretty much ignore the decoys, start tossing his bumper (which he's really excited about fetching) through them. He should completely ignore the decoys and tear off after the bumper. Continue to expose your young pup to decoys until he completely ignores them and will drive right through a small spread of them to fetch a bumper that has been tossed beyond. With the checkcord still on him, be sure to guide him back to you through the decoys, too, and don't let him get away with taking a detour around the spread.

And one more thing: Don't forget to incorporate a blank pistol in many of your marks, especially when they're thrown by a helper. Your dog needs to get used to the fact that gunfire is part of the fetching process. But wait until he's shown skill in his retrieves; don't add gunfire when he's still a young pup or while he's learning something new.

Handling

One of the greatest joys in training a retriever is to get him to the point where you can direct his movements from a distance. In response to your hand and voice signals, the dog will go where you want him to—*handling*. More than just show, handling is one of the most vital skills a retriever can learn; trainer Butch Goodwin explains why: "In a true hunting situation, most handling occurs when a dog has mismarked a fall or when the bird is seen swimming off or floating down a river. Unlike in trials and hunt tests, there are no ribbons or titles to be won and no gallery of spectators to judge the dog's performance—the only reward is recovering a dead or crippled bird."

With that said, let's discuss training a retriever to handle to retrieves, keeping in mind that these skills are taught after basic obedience is very solid, the dog is proficient at marks and he continues to show a high desire to retrieve.

The Baseball Drill

Teaching a retriever to handle is best accomplished with the Baseball Drill, which has been used in retriever-training circles for decades. Imagine the infield of a baseball diamond; the dog will always begin at the pitcher's mound, the handler will always be at home plate, and the two will always face each other. You'll handle your dog from the remote sitting position—that is, you've whistled the dog to sit while he was out in the field, and the dog turned around and sat down, facing you. Until the dog becomes very proficient at handling, bumpers should be kept at the positions of first, second and third base; as his skills improve, you can start adding angles. First and third bases require an "over" command, second base is picked up with a "back" command, and a bumper located between the dog and the handler uses the "in" command. These directions are called *casts*.

The bumpers should be placed several feet from the dog, on short grass—you don't want the dog to

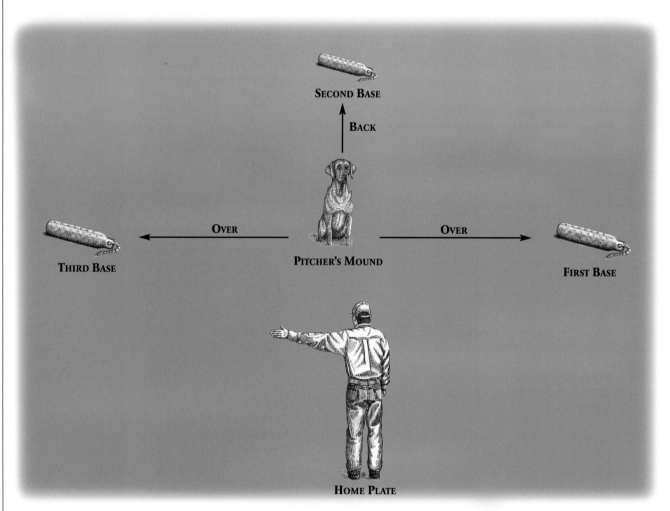

SECOND BASE

BACK

OVER

OVER

THIRD BASE

PITCHER'S MOUND

FIRST BASE

HOME PLATE

In the beginning, the baseball drill may seem complicated. But when mastered, the concepts will be used again and again.

fail because of either distance or cover. Use bright white bumpers on low grass a short distance away so that the dog can see everything that's going on.

Over. With the dog on a checkcord to give you some control if needed, walk the dog on "heel" out to the pitcher's mound, turn him around to face home plate and put him in a "sit" and "stay." At this point, there are no bumpers on the ground. Walk back to home plate, turn and face the dog; let things settle for a moment. Toss one white bumper to first base, making sure the dog sees it the whole way. He must be reliable with the "stay" command to resist the temptation to break and fetch the bumper; if he does break, walk out and take the bumper from him, place him back on the pitcher's mound and repeat the process until you toss the bumper to first base and he remains sitting. It may help to reinforce "stay" as you throw the bumper and when it lands. He may turn his butt to face the bumper; at this point, that's fine.

Get the dog's attention, either by snapping your fingers or clapping your hands once, keeping your hands together in the middle of your chest. This is one place where the "here" command is valuable; if you've taught it, go ahead and use it. Just prior to every cast you give, command, "Here!" to snatch your dog's focus. Eventually, the dog will seek out eye contact without the command, knowing that the sooner he settles down and pays attention, the quicker he'll be on his way to the retrieve.

When the dog has his eyes on you, stick your right hand flat out to the right side (the 3 o'clock position) as you take a giant step in that direction, saying, "Over." The dog may hesitate to go because up to this point, he's only ever been sent on his name. Just give another "over," or perhaps tie his name to the beginning of the command: "Rex— over!" After awhile, you can begin to phase out his name and just use "Over."

With a dog that has a high desire to retrieve, it shouldn't take much encouragement to get him to fetch the bumper at this new command. Have him bring the bumper back to you at home plate. Don't worry about sloppy deliveries at this point; they'll be cleaned up with the force-fetch exercise. Praise him for a job well done, take him back on "heel" to the pitcher's mound and repeat.

Be sure to exaggerate what you want, both verbally and physically. Goodwin says, "If your dog has trouble understanding the concept of fetching to the right or to the left from the sitting position, try using a great deal of body English to influence him to move in the direction that you want him to go. At this point, we are trying to give him the idea that he should fetch in the direction that he is cast. Don't demand absolute perfection at this early stage; instead, try to influence him to perform correctly and get the idea of what you want."

Now throw a bumper to third base. With your palm flat to the dog, move your left arm and hand into the 9 o'clock position and step to the left while you say, "Over," again. "Over" is used for a lateral cast in either direction; the direction the dog goes depends on where you point. So make sure that you use your arm and step in the direction you want the dog to go just before saying the "over" command, otherwise, the dog might not see you and might turn the way he wants.

For several days, work on these first- and third-base "overs," and make certain to praise the dog for good executions. Do not correct harshly at this point; simply stop the dog and start over if he goes in the wrong direction. Your checkcord will help with this. Keep the sessions short and recognize when the dog is beginning to lose interest. Don't forget to do some regular marks at the beginning or end of each session, and end on a positive note.

Accentuate an "over" by stepping in that direction. Make the movement exaggerated so the dog is sure to understand it.

Back. This cast is one of the most important that you'll ever teach your dog. If he's good at taking a straight line, he'll be able to get pretty close to a bird, even when things such as wind or ditches or other factors pull him off course. He may get out there and see a wing flap or catch scent and then zero in on the bird. But a lot of hunting dogs can have trouble carrying a straight line for a great distance. A common problem is that they'll *pop*; that is, they'll stop on their own and turn around to look at us for direction. A "back" command will tell the dog that the bird is behind him, that he must spin around and keep going; it will force the dog to carry his hunt out to greater distances.

Back on your small baseball infield, return the dog to the pitcher's mound and go back to home plate. Toss a bumper over the dog's head to second base. The dog may turn around to watch the bumper fall yet still remain sitting. If so, walk out to the dog and use your checkcord or his collar to turn him back around to face you at home plate. When you get back to home plate, he'll probably

alternate between looking at you and glancing over his shoulder at the bumper he desperately wants to pick up. Get his attention again, and when you've got it, raise either hand straight up over your head to the 12 o'clock position, palm flat, and say, "Back!" He should spin and get the bumper; use his name if necessary to get him going. Then use the "come" command or the checkcord to get him back to you.

In. I use the "in" command to get the dog to fetch something that's between us. Many people just blow the "come" whistle to get their dog moving toward them; the dog will then come across the bird or bumper and pick it up. However, I've found that a separate command, with an arm cast straight down to the ground (off to the side of your body so that the dog can see it) tends to focus the dog on the fact that there is something between you and that he isn't supposed to just return to your side. After all, when told to "come," he should properly do so without doing anything else, such as picking up a bird on the way.

So just as you've done with the other directions, begin with the dog on the pitcher's mound and you at home plate. Toss a white bumper into the air so that it lands right between the two of you. With your dog's attention on you, command, "In," and cast your arm down to the 6 o'clock position. By this time, the dog has learned that there are several commands used to get him to fetch, and he should leap off his feet and pick up the bumper.

Now that you have four places you can throw bumpers and direct the dog to, it comes down to lots of repetitions. It is best to do them one at a time; after some reliability is established, begin throwing two bumpers to two different bases, and then three, and then four (after several days of work). Be ready for the instant the dog turns to fetch a bumper you didn't indicate. Stop him with the cord or whistle; take him back to the beginning and recast to the bumper you want him to pick up. Again, don't expect perfect deliveries until after the force-fetch phase; and after you are through force-fetching, it's a good idea to go back to the simple, short fetches in the Baseball Drill to reemphasize proper delivery.

The "back" signal should be an arm straight up to the 12 o'clock position.

Angle Back. After days or weeks of working on the two "overs," "back" and "in," it's time to start refining your dog's handling skills. You'll now train the dog to spin over the proper shoulder to go "back," depending on which arm you raise. Why? Butch Goodwin has the answer: "You use the left and right 'back' casts to turn the dog away from 'suction' [such as a shoreline] that he might be heading toward, to correct the direction in which he is heading, or perhaps to cast him away from a dead bird lying on the water when you want him to go after a cripple that is swimming away. Trust me, you will use left- and right-hand 'back' casts regularly, and you will be glad that you taught the dog to turn in both directions from the start."

A perfect example of such a situation happened to me last season. Two birds were on the water, and two dogs were in the blind. K.D. went for a crippled duck that was actually closer to where Josie and I were hunting, while the other bird was being quickly blown out to the middle of the lake. Josie hadn't seen either bird fall. I sent her on a line toward the drifting duck as K.D. zeroed in on the crippled bird. But K.D. and the crippled bird were between Josie and the drifting duck. Josie watched as K.D. chased down the crippled bird and snatched it as it tried to flap past her. Josie turned around and looked at me as though to say, *Now what? She's got the bird.*

I sent her "back," but I could see that Josie was thinking I wanted her to take the duck from K.D. As she swam toward K.D., I stopped her with a hard whistle blast and sent her "back" again, only in the opposite direction from K.D. She spun over her right shoulder, away from the other dog. As a result, she didn't see K.D. or the duck even when they were very close to her, where she could have been tempted to try to grab the duck. Once Josie was beyond K.D., I stopped her again and gave her another "back" over her left shoulder; she spun and saw the drifting duck. Game over.

To teach the dog this valuable skill, begin on the baseball infield again, but when you toss the bumper over the dog's head, angle it to land halfway between first and second base. This will encourage the dog to turn around over the proper shoulder. If he turns his body when you throw the bumper, you'll have to square him up so that he's facing you entirely.

To teach the dog to go "back" over the proper shoulder, start with the bumper halfway between the bases, which will force the dog to go over the corrct shoulder. Eventually work so the bumper is again at second base.

When you give the verbal "Back!" command and cast, use your right hand, but raise your arm to the 2 o'clock position instead of 12 o'clock. Step in that direction, too, but not as far as you do when giving the "over" cast to first base. If the dog turns over his right shoulder (which would mean he would be facing between second and third base), stop him, bring him back to the pitcher's mound and repeat. Only when he turns over the proper shoulder should he be allowed to make the retrieve.

Flop this procedure around for teaching the other angle. Throw the bumper so that it lands between second and third base—at shortstop—and use your left hand at 10 o'clock with the "back" command to get the dog to spin over his right shoulder. Keep the "back" angles wide at first. As the dog masters spinning correctly in response to your arm, begin to tighten the angle behind him. Eventually, you want to land the bumper at second base and have the dog turn over the proper shoulder depending on which arm you raise to the 12 o'clock position. Whenever he spins over the wrong shoulder, stop him and start again from the beginning.

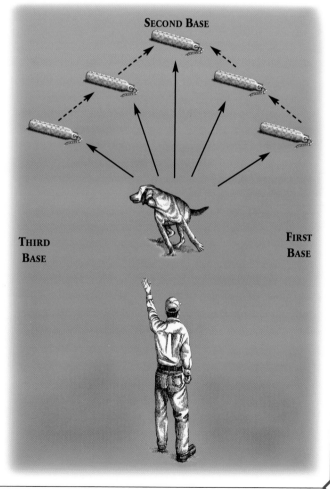

SECOND BASE

THIRD BASE

FIRST BASE

Now it's just a matter of repetitions, increasing distances after a reliable delivery is established and changing locations and cover types. Goodwin offers a last piece of advice for proper casting technique so that you don't confuse the dog: "Most casting problems later on are a direct result of the handler's sloppiness when giving arm and hand signals. An 'over' cast is not a sweep of the arm up from the crotch and out to the side; it is straight out from the solar plexus. Likewise, a 'back' cast is not akin to a Nazi salute with the arm coming forward; it is straight up from the solar plexus to the side of the left or right eye." He suggests practicing in front of a mirror to see if you're casting correctly.

You've started your dog down the road to becoming a handling retriever, and these skills will become your greatest asset when he is sent on a retrieve and loses his way. Always cast him toward a bumper so that he learns he can trust you to point him in the right direction.

The "T" Drill

This basic casting drill is very valuable in that it reinforces and combines a number of skills you've been working on up to this point; it also builds the trust your dog has in you and his confidence in running nice long lines. Evan Graham says, "We are usually dealing with a youngster around eight months to a year of age at this point of training." Once a dog is very proficient with the Baseball Drill and can handle to multiple bumpers around him, start with the T Drill to combine lots of skills.

The best way to think of the T Drill is as a Baseball Drill with both you and the dog at home plate. You'll cast the dog on a line to second base, stop him with a whistle sit at the pitcher's mound and then cast him to first, second or third base. The paths the dog needs to cover will be made more visible to him if you can cut lanes in an unmowed yard in the shape of a small letter "t," or more correctly, a cross.

Instead of single bumpers at various positions, you'll use piles of bumpers at each base. Sending a

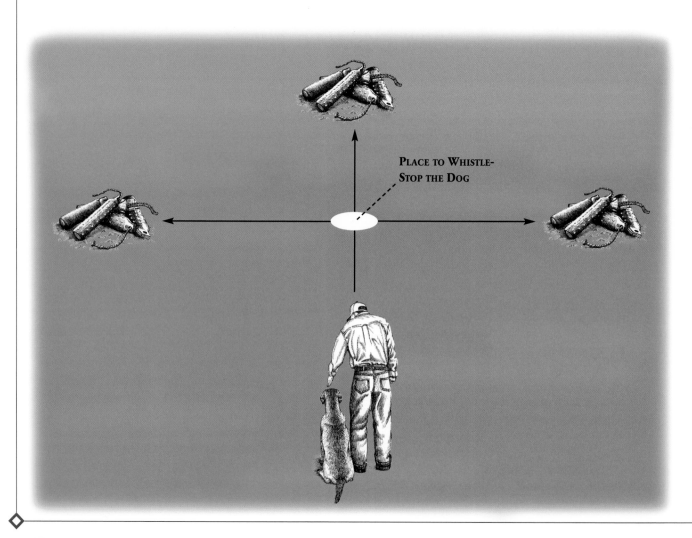

PLACE TO WHISTLE-
STOP THE DOG

dog to a pile of bumpers is a good way to sharpen lining skills. Because you're repeatedly sending the dog to the same spot to fetch multiple bumpers, he quickly learns to trust the path you send him on. Sending a young dog to a pile also increases the odds that he'll succeed in finding what he's after because there are more objects out there.

Before beginning the T Drill, do some preliminary pile work on a simple straight line, where the dog goes out to the same spot repeatedly for fetches. Identify the pile by sitting him a short distance away and putting him on "stay." Walk out in front of him and throw the bumpers clearly in his line of sight so that he can see them fall and land; they should land in a pile. (This is a good, quick way to get lots of bumpers out in one spot.) Then walk the dog on "heel" back to the spot where you want to start him, line him up, send him on his name to the marked retrieve and continue to send him until all of the bumpers have been picked up.

When he's comfortable working with a single pile, sit him on the pitcher's mound and identify a pile at each of the bases. (Each pile need contain only a few bumpers at this point.) Take him back to home plate, line him up to second base and send him. The mowed path to second base will help him carry the line. If you find that he's not taking a straight line but is instead doing a wide curve to the pile, shorten the distance between you and the pile.

Once the dog reaches the intersection of the "t" (i.e., the pitcher's mound), whistle-stop him, give him the "here" command to get his attention on you, and cast to the base of your choice. Keep the checkcord on him to make sure that he obeys the whistle sit immediately and that he delivers the bumper back to you instead of checking out the other piles. Here's where the pile concept comes in handy—there are already a number of bumpers in position, so you don't have to rethrow.

Send the dog again toward the second-base pile, stop him on the pitcher's mound and cast again; don't neglect the importance of sending him on a "back" toward second base, which is where he was going in the first place. This exercise helps to reinforce the "back" cast.

As with the Baseball Drill, you may find that the

dog pops—stopping and sitting on his own without a command, in this case at the pitcher's mound. So don't forget to occasionally let the dog run all the way to the second base pile without stopping him.

If the dog does pop, I usually give him the "back" cast the first few times to let him know, "Yes, keep going in that direction." If popping starts to become a habit, call the dog back to your side, reline him and send him again. If he pops again, bring him back with a "come," reline him and send him again until he goes all the way to second base. If you start seeing popping behavior repeatedly, get a few good solid lines to second base out of your dog, then quit. You want the dog to assume that you're lining him where you want him to go, unless you decide to stop him with the whistle. He is to keep running until you say to stop.

Graham says, "Combined with polishing basic casting and stopping skills, these [T Drills] prepare a young dog for smooth advancement [and] transition to a cold blind standard." Now that your dog has a firm grasp on taking a straight line, stopping when you say so and following your directions to a retrieve, that's where we'll go—to blind retrieves.

Blind Retrieves

Simply defined, a blind retrieve is one in which the dog did not see the bumper fall or has forgotten the location of the bumper on the ground—it is "blind" to him. In this instance, it is up to you to direct the dog to the bumper using a proper line, a whistle and handling skills. A successful blind retrieve depends entirely upon the skills and trust you have developed with your dog.

Being able to execute blind retrieves is one of the most vital skills for the hunting retriever. If you hunt from a boat or a shore blind, many—probably most—of the dog's retrieves will not be marks. He won't see what's going on, only that you've shot at something; and he may or may not see the duck among the decoys on the water once you get him out of the boat or blind to line him up. The dog must trust your directions and casts and not ignore commands if you are to put him in the correct position to recover the bird.

Building this trust and reliable obedience to your

The T-drill combines many skills: taking a proper line, whistle-stop and handling.

directions and commands will take patience on your part. "Unlike basic marking, running blinds is not a natural function," says Evan Graham. "That's not to say that certain aspects of the work aren't influenced by instinct or intuition. But running in a direction where the dog has seen nothing fall, then stopping to the whistle and taking casts, represents an entirely unnatural set of events for a dog to participate in."

So be patient, go slow and reinforce lining and handling skills until they are very sound. (Your first attempts at blind retrieves will show you whether your dog is truly unfailing at lining and handling.) Let the dog use his nose once you put him in the right position—the "dead bird" command is very useful for helping cue the dog that he's in the right spot.

When you start out teaching blind retrieves, don't correct too harshly lest you dampen your dog's enthusiasm for going confidently in the direction you send him. "The mechanical components of training needed to do [blind retrieves] dictate that this is an older dog with more experience and knowledge of his basic skills," Graham says. "Being an unnatural function, blinds should be carefully introduced to keep corrections confined to supporting only the basic functions of go-stop-come. The command for these functions should be well in place before the first actual blind retrieve is attempted, in my view. When a correction is needed to support these basic functions, it should be only in an amount required to gain an appropriate response."

In other words, keep corrections to the very minimum that is needed to gain compliance, and correct only the skills you're certain the dog knows. When in doubt, hold your correction and simply stop the dog from doing

The blind retrieve shows how much trust your dog has in you and how well he's mastered his lining and handling skills.

the wrong behavior; then start over the right way.

When I attempted my first blind retrieve with Josie, I threw the bumper as a mark in short grass and let her look at it on the ground. Then we did a lot of different things—we worked on obedience in a different area; I threw her some other marks in a different direction; we played a little bit. Then I lined her up toward the original white bumper—she had now forgotten where it had fallen, though it was clear she thought she could see it on the ground. I lined her up and sent her on the word "Back!" instead of her name. (Use this word on every blind retrieve; the dog will eventually learn that it means he is heading out to fetch something that he didn't see. Being sent on the dog's name is for marked retrieves.)

Her lining skills were reliable, and she carried a straight line for about 20 or 30 yards before starting to veer off. I let her go until she was even with the bumper but far off to the right. Then I whistle-stopped her and gave her an "over" cast; she followed it right to the bumper, spotting it on the ground easily. With lots of repetitions of these types of blind retrieves, she began to understand that sometimes she would be sent for fetches that she hadn't recently seen fall.

This type of exercise helps to build trust between the dog and handler and further refines whistle commands, handling skills and lining skills. If you have a perfect lining retriever, there should be no need for handling—the dog will continue on the proper course you point him in until he comes across the bumper. But any number of things called "factors" can affect the dog's line: wind direction, terrain (ditches, slopes, hills), cover or obstacles (logs, hunting blinds, trees, bushes). These factors will naturally pull the dog off line, thus the need for a good whistle sit and obedience to casts that will put him back on the proper line.

Once the dog is doing simple blind retrieves effectively, start tossing in some *cold blinds*—retrieves in which the dog has no knowledge whatsoever that a bumper is out there to be fetched. At first, use white bumpers so that the dog can use his eyes as well as his nose to search; once he's experienced, switch to blaze-orange bumpers (which dogs cannot see nearly as well) so that he must practice using his nose to locate the fetch.

The easiest way to do a cold blind is to throw a long mark and send the dog out to fetch it; once the dog is on his way, turn around 180 degrees and throw another bumper. He won't see it. Once he delivers the first bumper, turn him around to this cold blind, line him up (using a "here" command if necessary), and give him a "Back!" Expect some hesitation at first, but he should have enough experience to know that he doesn't always need to see a bumper fall in order to find something to fetch. Direct him with the whistle and casts to the bumper, and you've just completed your first cold blind.

Repetition of blind retrieves is one of the best things you can do to build your dog's confidence in you as a handler. Just remember to never send him anywhere or give any kind of cast unless there is something to be fetched at the other end. For extreme diversions from the proper line, you may need to give an "over" to get back to the line, and then a "back" to go back to the bumper; but an angle-back cast might work just as well if the dog can turn over the proper shoulder.

Once your dog is doing simple cold blinds efficiently, you can plant bumpers in heavier cover—or use orange bumpers—while he's still in the house or kennel and cannot see you. Make sure you have a landmark on each bumper's proper line so that you send the dog in the right direction. I plant bumpers at the base of a shrub or a small tree, or if they're in the open, I stick a small orange flag in the ground that I can see from a distance.

Bring the dog out, do a little obedience, throw a couple of marks to get the juices flowing and line him up at the blind. By this time, he should know that there is something to be fetched out there. With the "here" command to prompt him to look down your hand at the proper line, he should take off in search of the fetch you have just promised him.

Make sure to pour on the praise for a job well done with blind retrieves because your retriever has just put together all of the skills he'll need to become a finished, reliable hunting partner: He paid attention to the line, followed spoken and whistle commands, followed hand signals, demonstrated the drive to hunt out something he had no clue was out there and enthusiastically returned to your side.

Advanced Drills and Skills

Of course, you aren't done once the dog has displayed a consistent level of accomplishment with marks and blinds and handling–at least not if you want to be thoroughly confident that your dog is the effective and efficient hunter you've always wanted. Many retriever-training books contain all sorts of drills and setups for testing a dog in many situations–whether you'll use them or not depends entirely upon the kind of hunting you do and whether you might encounter these situations. But there are some advanced skills that every finished hunting retriever should know.

Force-Fetch

It may seem odd to think that you have to teach a retriever to retrieve, but that's just what this vital exercise does. It makes the fetching process a command that can be enforced should the dog decide not to comply. For example, a dog will sit naturally, but we still teach him the "sit" command for those times when we want him to sit even if he doesn't feel like it. His understanding of the corrections associated with noncompliance gives us tools to enforce the command should he choose to disobey–a pull up on his collar, a push down on his rump, a single whistle blast.

Force-fetch is exactly the same: Though a retriever will naturally carry things around in his mouth and bring them to you, what recourse would you have to correct him and insist upon his delivery of the item if he fetches only when he felt like it? By going through the process of force-fetch, you give yourself a way to enforce the fetching behavior by adding two commands to the process, "hold" and "fetch." This is also the best way to drill the "give" command, which you've been saying every time you've taken something from the dog's mouth. These commands will ensure that the dog will pick up anything you tell him to and hold it in his mouth until you are ready to take it from him. No more sloppy deliveries where the dog drops the bumper when he's still on his way back to your side. With force-fetch, you'll put the finishing touches on a clean delivery right to the "heel" position. And as odd as it may seem, the dog ends up even more enthusiastic about retrieving than he was before he was forced.

But before we continue, here's a warning: This is a difficult procedure to teach, and it can be challenging. Your dog's temperament will have much to do with how fast you can proceed through the exercise; it may take as little as a few days to as long as several months to finish this skill. You'll need a very calm and even temperament–not too firm and not too mushy–and you'll need to exert as much patience as you've got.

Always keep force-fetch sessions short, 5 to 10 minutes. In the meantime, suspend all other retrieving work: You don't want the dog to think that he can be sloppy everywhere except when he's being taught "hold" and "fetch." But you won't yet have educated him on the proper way to hold and fetch; you won't be able to enforce these new commands. So stop all other fetching exercises; instead, take the dog on walks and work on obedience.

Many people have a hard time teaching this skill because it involves inflicting a small amount of discomfort on the dog. For this reason, it is highly recommended that you thoroughly research this process with several training sources; the best way to learn is to have a professional trainer–or at the very least, a friend who has finished this process before–teach you hands-on. You can get the main idea of how the process is taught from what follows, but understand that in this one chapter there is no way to address all the avoidance behaviors (and how to deal with them) that your dog may perform. So talk to lots of people, consider consulting a professional trainer and confer with many training sources. This is one skill for which an instructional training video is extremely valuable.

You'll want to wait to teach your dog to force-fetch until all of his adult teeth have come in. Do not try this exercise while he still has his puppy teeth– his mouth will be plenty sensitive and painful to begin with, and he won't like being manipulated in that area. So around 6 to 9 months, after his adult chompers have come in (not *while* they're coming in), you can start this vital exercise. It might help to think of this process as eight steps toward the goal.

Step One. The dog must first "sit" and "stay" very well; place him up on top of his crate and give him the commands. Being on top of his crate limits his movement options, and it helps spare your back from bending over all the time. Gently open his mouth and insert a bumper, reminding him to stay if he tries to get up. Once the bumper is in his mouth, help him keep it closed by gently pressing his jaws together. As you do so, command, "Hold" in a nice, even, pleasant tone. While you're holding his mouth together with one hand, gently pet him with the other, repeating, "Hold." Then roll the bumper backward down his mouth as you say, "Give." This maneuver will force the dog to open his mouth very wide; take the bumper, praise him on the give and pet him up.

Repeat this procedure for a few sessions and begin to decrease the pressure you exert on his jaws to keep his mouth around the bumper, allowing him to hold the bumper himself. Always say your commands in a smooth tone, and gently take the bumper with the "give" command. You usually won't have problems with this part, as the dog will be more than happy to give up the bumper.

Step Two. As the dog begins to get better and better at holding the bumper, place one hand under his chin, grasping his fur with a couple fingers and pushing up instead of clamping his jaws shut. You will tap in this location as a reminder to the dog to "hold" as you progress. Eventually, all you'll have to do is press upward with one finger in this location, and the dog will solidify his hold on the bumper.

After several "hold" sessions, start stepping away, taking your hands away from the dog's mouth and letting him hold the bumper on his own. If he attempts to drop it, say, "No," grasp and reinsert the bumper in his mouth, and repeat the "hold" command with a tap under the chin. Let him hold the bumper a few seconds, then take it with a "give" command.

Step Three. Once the dog is reliably holding the bumper (which can take several days), take him off the crate and move him to different locations. Let him walk at "heel" while he's holding the bumper; have him sit and hold for an extended period of time; go through other obedience commands such as the "sit-stay-come-heel" routine, where he comes and sits at your side while holding the bumper. Have him hold different objects, too. Only when the "hold" command is solid should you move on to teaching the "fetch" command.

A tap under the chin will reinforce the "hold" command.

Once the dog has "hold" mastered, do some basic obedience training while the dog holds the bumper.

The ear pinch is the pressure the dog will learn to turn off by grasping the bumper. As soon as it's in his mouth, release the pinch.

It's very important that you move these skills to the ground so that the dog learns he is to pick up anything–anywhere– on command.

Step Four. At this point, return the dog to the top of the crate, since he's learning something new. You may notice the dog starting to open his mouth on his own when he sees you bringing the bumper toward his face. If so, count yourself lucky–teaching the "fetch" command will be a snap. But if you still have to open his mouth to insert the bumper, do so now while saying, "Fetch." Then progress through the "hold" and "give" portions of the procedure as you've been doing. Keep repeating "fetch" every time you insert the bumper; but again, start "fetch" only after you've taught "hold"–you want your dog to learn only one new thing at a time.

Step Five. Now it's time to add pressure in the form of an ear pinch or a toe hitch. I prefer the ear pinch because it will be easier to employ in the field than hitching a thin rope around the dog's toes. Pinch the dog's ear flap hard enough to make it uncomfortable–don't worry, you won't hurt his ear. But the dog will begin to yelp in pain; when he opens his mouth to vocalize his discomfort, insert the bumper and say, "Fetch." As soon as the bumper is in his mouth, release the ear pinch, give the "hold" command, stroke the dog gently and tell him how good he is. Use a "give" command to take the bumper, and really praise him up.

Some tough dogs may take quite a bit of pressure to get them to open their mouths–you may even have to pinch the ear against the buckle of his collar–but be persistent and don't let up until the bumper is in there. Limit your initial ear-pinch sessions to only a few repetitions; then quit and do something fun with the dog, such as taking him for a walk.

You might be amazed at how quickly some dogs will figure out that the way to turn the pressure off is to take the bumper. Some dogs will cooperate after only four or five ear-pinch sessions, with only a few pinches in each session. Others may take several weeks, especially dominant male dogs.

Step Six. Once the dog readily takes the bumper upon being pinched, give him some freebies, instances where you only say, "Fetch," to see if he'll reach out and take the bumper. The ear pinch becomes the reinforcement of the "fetch" command, much like a light swat on the rump becomes a reminder to "sit." So hold the bumper in front of his mouth; don't let him take it until you say "Fetch," and praise him when he takes it.

Let him hold it as you repeat the "hold" command, pet him up and use a "give" to release.

Occasionally say the command and immediately pinch his ear–this will get him to actively take the bumper in an attempt to "beat the pinch." He's thinking that if he grabs the bumper quickly upon the command, there won't be a need for you to pinch. And he's right.

Step Seven. Now begin to move the bumper farther away from his mouth; he should be reaching for it at this point when you say the "fetch" command. If he doesn't, pinch his ear and keep the bumper in place–make him come to it. Gradually move it lower and lower to the ground–the whole purpose of this command is to get the dog to pick up something off the ground at our command. At first, the dog will have trouble with this, so keep your fingers on the bumper while it's on the ground, maybe even lifting up the edge to identify what you want him to pick up. Begin to phase out help as he becomes more and more reliable.

Step Eight. Now it's time to test the dog further, once he's very proficient at fetching and holding on command and you don't have to pinch his ear anymore. Scatter several bumpers on the ground, and with the dog on a leash and at heel, walk him around the bumpers. If he moves toward a bumper when you didn't give him the "fetch" command, tell him, "No," and give him a slight tap with the leash to keep him moving. At one bumper, command, "Fetch." He should lean down to pick it up. Once he has it, keep walking with him at heel while you give him the "hold" command. When it comes time to take the bumper, stop, have him sit, and reach down and take the bumper with a "give" command. After that it is constant repetition.

One note on the "give" command: Once the dog is reliable, he should only give you the bumper when you say the command. He shouldn't spit it out at your moving hand if you haven't said, "Give." Test this by tapping the bumper while it's in the dog's mouth, saying "Hold" all the while. Eventually grab one end of the bumper while it's in his mouth and keep your hand there; only when you say "Give" do you take it. Also, if you have a reluctant giver, open his mouth and take the bumper from him the same way you opened it to insert the bumper.

This entire process, as stated earlier, can take a few days or several weeks or months. In any case, it is not to be rushed. Your dog will look very sheepish during this time, and you'll worry that you're killing his retrieving drive. But he'll come out of it as a more intense retriever, now with solid mouth habits.

In Conclusion. Professional retriever trainers John and Amy Dahl of Oak Hill Kennel in Pinehurst, North Carolina, sum up the process best by saying, "Making 'fetch' a command that your dog clearly understands leads to greater confidence than is possible otherwise. When training becomes confusing or stressful [perhaps the dog is corrected for going to the wrong place, or for breaking], the dog's understanding of the fetch command provides a way out of the confusion, a resolution to the stress. The dog knows that completing the retrieve is the right thing to do. While the prospect of systematically applying pressure [pain] to a pet is unappealing to most owners, force-fetching is far more humane in the long run than is neglecting to do so. The unpleasantness to a dog of being confused, knowing something is expected but not knowing what, must not be underestimated. Most dogs seem much more distressed at this kind of confusion than they are by moderate pain applied in a straightforward manner. By force-fetching, and by fair, step-by-step training following force-fetching, you give your dog the power to avoid confusion and 'turn off' pressure." This, incidentally, is the primary principle behind the electronic collar–the dog learns how to turn off the pressure by following our commands.

Go back to basics in your marking, starting off with simple marks, and enjoy watching the dog bring the bumper all the way to the "heel" position to await your taking it from him. When he's getting near you, tell him, "Hold," to remind him, and then guide him into the delivery position. Progress through all of the drills and handling and marks and blinds you've been doing up to this point, starting over at the beginning, and correct him with an ear pinch or a tap under the chin if he drops the bumper–he now knows better.

As stated earlier, do lots of research on this procedure and get lots of advice before embarking on it. "Hold" and "fetch" are two of the most useful commands you can teach your dog, and they'll help him become the solid, dependable retriever you want.

Taking an Honest Line

You've been working very hard at getting your retriever to take a straight line on a retrieve, and you should expect this standard during all of his training. But in a lot of hunting situations, many hunters allow their dogs to "cheat." This most often refers to the tendency of some dogs to search out an alternate route to a bird or bumper on the water by running along the shoreline, jumping into the water at a strategic point to shorten the swim to the bird, getting back out onto shore and running back to the hunter's side. Some dogs take this approach instead of swimming a long straight line right at the bird or bumper.

Try to dissuade this cheating behavior right from the start. John and Amy Dahl say that a retriever that will take a straight, honest line on a fetch instead of being allowed to cheat has many advantages. Among them are better marking skills (the dog won't lose the bird while trying to find an alternate route) and a better attitude (the dog will take obstacles in stride and maintain his drive and

focus). The dog that takes a straight line will also avoid cover on shore, which can easily confuse and delay him, as well as dangers such as traps, fences, cattle, etc.

"Teaching a dog to go straight is not a matter of a drill or two, but of establishing the habit throughout training," say the Dahls. "Early in training, the focus is to avoid teaching the dog that there is an easy way, by throwing marks where the straight path is obvious and alternatives are not. This means working straight out into the water or running from a point so the straight route affords the shortest possible swim to the bird."

When you are confident in your dog's ability to take a solid straight line, start to test him. "You can set up some cheating temptations using a helper to haze him off the shore. These should be simple marks, as the shore training will distract him from marking. The helper should have a stick or a pole to fend the dog off the shore, but without frightening or intimidating him. If the dog lands and tries to run the shore on the return, the helper should take the dummy and throw it into the water where the dog should be returning. This lesson can be repeated a number of times in different settings, ideally until the dog will swim end to end in a relatively long, narrow pond or channel."

Having a retriever that you can handle will give you the tools to correct cheating behavior; this is also a good spot for attrition training–stopping the dog that is performing a wrong behavior, bringing him back and starting again. "Any time the dog sets out on a devious route," continue the Dahls, "stop him with the whistle. Either cast him in the correct direction or call him back to try again." This would mean stopping the dog as he runs along the shoreline, giving him an "over" to get him back into the water, then casting him "back" so that he swims to the bumper.

But if you start from the beginning in expecting your dog to run in the direction you line him, he'll learn that there is one way to do things. "Dogs do what works. If yours learns that attempting to run around only creates a delay, he will give it up. If you let him succeed some of the time, however, he'll continue to gamble that this time he may get away with it–so consistency is essential."

The shortest distance between two points is a straight line—something your dog must learn and remember.

A difficult skill for some dogs to master is that of reentering the water after making a retrieve on land.

Land-Water-Land Retrieves

If you waterfowl hunt in pothole country or in marshy areas, you may find that sometimes a duck or goose is dropped on the shore opposite where you're hunting. To retrieve such a bird, your dog must leap from the land blind, swim across the water and get back up onto shore to find the bird that tumbled onto land. If you might encounter this scenario, it pays big dividends to practice it in the off-season.

John and Amy Dahl provide some helpful tips for exposing your retriever to this new situation. "Make the retrieve short and obvious, and make sure there is no temptation to cheat. Set up a mark across a narrow channel, and run from a spot close to shore. Using a visible thrower on the far shore and making sure the throw is readily visible against the background helps the dog see the far shore as the destination." They recommend using large white bumpers and landing the bumper in low cover so that the mark is clearly visible.

The most common problem in these types of retrieves, according to the Dahls, is "the dog's not wanting to get into the water again on the return. It is a good idea to start blowing the come-in whistle insistently as soon as the dog gets to the dummy. Sometimes a long checkcord is necessary–not to haul the dog back but to guide him into the water for the return." That is, don't let your dog cheat by running the shoreline all around the pond to come back to you–a straight line is the quickest path.

The same rules apply if you're asking the dog to start out in water, swim to land and cross it, and then reenter the water on the opposite side for a fetch. Make it painstakingly obvious where he must go for the fetch, setting him up for countless chances of success before you add in difficult factors–such as distance, cover or blind retrieves. In these retrieves, the dog may have a tendency to hunt on the land and cheat back to you instead of taking a straight line back across the land and into the water.

Difficult Marks and Blinds

Of course, your dog will probably not find many of the birds he'll fetch during the hunting season lying in a mowed yard 20 yards away. Evan Graham rightly says, "I think it's important to realize that a hunting retriever should be prepared to encounter retrieves that involve all kinds of difficult challenges. You never know how far away the birds will fall. You cannot predict the presence of reentries, diversions, cover changes or any of the countless conceptual challenges that are common in the field or marsh on any given retrieve. With that in mind, anyone planning to hunt [his] dog would be well advised to prepare [the dog] for [his] life's work as thoroughly as possible." This means making your marked and blind retrieves more and more difficult.

For the most part, increasing difficulty means increasing distance and cover. It also means employing the help of a friend to throw retrieves so that you can focus on handling the dog; a helper will be able to go out quite a distance and throw retrieves beyond the 30 or 40 yards maximum that you can toss from your side.

So make the marks and blinds longer; use orange bumpers; go to public hunting land and take advantage of the heavier cover, changing terrain, tree belts and natural obstacles; train in stiffer winds; throw multiple retrieves that mimic situations your dog may encounter. For example, throw one bumper on the water; while the dog is on his way, toss another one so that it lands close to his line, symbolizing a late duck that got shot. Then stop and cast the dog to your choice. Graham suggests, "Create concepts in places they don't naturally exist. This may start with using what is present in more creative ways, such as running from different angles across a ditch or log. Drag logs or hay bales around to alter the concept presentation." Pull out any and all stops to make your marks and blinds as difficult as the hardest fetch you think your dog will ever encounter.

But don't just pluck your retriever out of the yard or clear pond, plop him in flooded timber in gale-force winds and expect him to drive through the shrubs to a bumper 100 yards away. Introduce new and challenging factors one at a time. Take advantage of a windy day to introduce this factor in the yard on short marks and blinds, making sure to use a heavily scented bumper. On a calm, clear day, increase distances to 100 or 200 yards. Introduce a ditch or obstacles when those will be the only new things the dog will have to deal with.

Once he starts getting the hang of how to deal with these factors, combine them—a long mark on a windy day; heavy cover or cover changes through a ditch or stream. This is the really fun part of training because you'll get to see your dog put all of his skills together and use his own confidence to execute some pretty difficult retrieves.

Once your dog has the skills, start increasing the difficulty of the retrieves. Throwing the bumper in thick cover is one easy way to do this.

When things break down, go back to basics on marks and blinds and handling and obedience, and eliminate those challenging factors one at a time until he's successful. Repetition of success builds confidence, and that confidence is what will carry the dog through the demanding conditions that actual hunting situations present. Keep track of what your dog encounters during the hunting season; do your best to re-create those situations in the off-season to better prepare him for the next year.

Calling Off a Retrieve

Unfortunately, many times you will not kill a duck outright. A crippled bird can present a retrieving challenge, and in questionable conditions, it could lead a dog into dangerous situations. Crippled ducks—both dabblers and divers—can dive under the water and pop up several to many yards away; a retriever, in his relentless pursuit, can quickly be swept into places that can threaten his safety.

For this reason—and because it is the humane thing to do—it is recommended that crippled ducks and geese be dispatched as quickly as possible by shooting them on the water. But the dog needs to be out of the line of fire, and a dog that has a tendency to break when he sees a bird fall will need to immediately "sit" at the whistle or voice to stay out of harm's way. The one-whistle blast should always be followed without hesitation, and it should be practiced until you get this reliability. Once the dog is sitting, a "come" command can bring him back to your side; you can then dispatch the duck and resend the dog.

Practice this technique by stopping the dog, bringing him back to your side, firing a blank gun and then resending him. Don't do it too often; otherwise you'll develop a dog that pops (stopping on his own as if he's unsure that you want him to go). But dealing with a little popping behavior is, in my opinion, acceptable if it leads to a dog that you can call off of a crippled bird. This ability will help you recover the bird and keep the dog out of danger—and it is the humane thing to do instead of allowing the dog to chase a mortally wounded animal. Be ready with the whistle—or better yet, reinforce steadiness on the shot and fall, and you won't have to worry about it.

Waterfowl Hunting Skills

Most retrievers will find their lives spent in a duck blind or boat instead of in the uplands. The former is what they were bred for, what they live and breathe—those frenetic plunges into icy waters in pursuit of ducks and geese. Sometimes I have a difficult time deciding whether our dogs' trembling in the boat is from the cold or from the excitement.

There are many different types of waterfowl hunting, and some require different sets of skills of the dog. Take a good look at what you like to do, and begin training for these skills early in your dog's life. That means training for them in actual hunting setups. Bring out the boats and blinds and

"Hold" takes on a whole new meaning when it's a duck and not a bumper.

decoys and tree stands and expose your dog to them. "Too often when training, we leave these items at home, and our retrievers only see them while hunting," says retriever trainer James Keldsen. "They then associate these items with the excitement of hunting, negatively affecting their behavior. If these items are a regular occurrence in everyday life, they lose some of their intoxicating effects. Learn a lesson from Pavlov and don't turn your hunting gear into a dinner bell."

The following are the essential sets of skills a retriever should know for each general type of waterfowl hunting.

In a Boat Blind. Basic obedience, with special emphasis on "sit" for boat rides and "come" if you must sacrifice a bird to keep the dog from endangering himself; unquestionable steadiness; remaining quiet; marks and blinds (up to about 200 yards); handling skills; being called off a crippled bird; solid delivery; perhaps the "spot" command if he has a designated place in the boat to sit; using a dog ladder for exit and entry on a retrieve.

In a Shore Blind. Basic obedience; solid steadiness; remaining quiet; marks and blinds (the distance depends on where you're hunting—consider the shore of a huge lake versus a prairie pothole); land-water-land retrieves; handling skills; being called off a crippled bird; solid delivery; experience with a river current if hunting along a river (angling downstream for retrieves, running back along the shore instead of fighting current—this is when running the shore is acceptable, but only on the way back—etc.).

In a Field Blind. Basic obedience, with special emphasis on "down" to remain still and low; steadiness; remaining quiet; marks and blinds (up to extreme distances to chase down "sailers"–crippled birds, especially geese, that can sail quite a distance); handling skills; solid delivery; experience with being covered up by some sort of tarp or burlap for camouflage.

Jump-shooting. Basic obedience, with special emphasis on "heel" so that the dog won't burst ahead and scare ducks, on "stay" and "down" so that he can remain in one place while you creep forward, and on "sit" so that he remains steady when you rise to shoot; marks and blinds (up to 100 yards); land-water-land retrieves; handling; being called off a crippled bird; solid delivery; experience with a river current if jump-shooting rivers.

Pass-shooting. Basic obedience, with special emphasis on "sit" and "stay" for remaining in one place for long periods of time; marks and blinds (up to extreme distances depending on where and what you're shooting); handling; solid delivery; experience with a river current if pass-shooting rivers.

Butch Goodwin also adds one more key ingredient for the solid waterfowl dog: "I consider the number-one waterfowl hunting skill to be self-confidence on the part of the dog. True hunting dogs are walking a very fine line between control from the handler and the self-confidence to think for themselves." Being able to sort things out for himself—and the handler letting him—is the polish on a dog's finished battery of hunter and retriever skills.

Solid steadiness is of utmost importance if your dog will be hunting from a blind.

You'll need the upland flusher in range if you want a shot at the bird.

Upland Hunting Skills

For the most part, all different types of upland hunting will require the same set of skills from a retriever—that of quartering within gun range, solid adherence to obedience commands, marking retrieves and delivering the bird nicely to the "heel" position. Whether you're hunting pheasants or quail or ruffed grouse or prairie chickens, you'll need your flushing retriever in range if you want a chance at the bird, and he'll need to effectively scour the cover.

That's done by quartering—the dog works ahead of you in a zigzag fashion and hunts in front of all the hunters if you have company. This can be a challenging skill to teach a dog that has remained at your side for his waterfowl training. You are now asking him to go on ahead and run around to find the birds that will (hopefully) produce the retrieves he desires.

Retriever trainer Charlie Jurney says to begin encouragement of a dog's instinctual desire to explore early on. "A long daily walk will reap multiple benefits for a young pup. Pup will want to go exploring, but it is unlikely that he will range too

far from you. As Pup is bounding around in front of you, start communicating to him that you like his actions with a happy, 'Hunt 'em up!'"

Quartering. Begin with your young puppy as soon as you bring him home. You can start right in the front yard, with the puppy on a checkcord for a measure of control, and simply let the dog romp ahead of you. If he runs back toward you and then past you, turn around so that when he looks back he sees your face. "Initially, your job is to follow him in whatever direction he goes. Pup must learn that his place is in front of you," says Jurney. You can always bring him to your side later on with a snappy "heel" command.

When your puppy starts to mature and likes these romps in the field, begin developing his range. Jurney explains, "On one of your daily walks with Pup, he will decide to venture off on his own. Pup is bold now and ready to challenge your authority, so be prepared when this happens. It is time to start incorporating some obedience into the quartering process. Use the 'here' [or 'come'] command to call

Pup back toward you each time he ventures too far. With enough repetition, Pup will learn how far he is allowed to stray while hunting." Jurney also recommends that you use the whistle at this time to help get the dog to respond to the "come" command.

Once the dog realizes about how far he is allowed to range in front of you–which should be in gun range, about 20 to 40 yards–you can start developing his pattern of quartering a field. "Start off by commanding Pup to 'Hunt 'em up!' When he goes out in one direction, you veer off in the other," says Jurney. "As he is about to turn on his own, give a 'tweet-tweet' on the whistle, causing him to turn and come toward you. When Pup looks up at you, hold out your arm, pointing in the direction you are heading. Start walking a zigzag pattern through the field on your daily treks. If Pup zigs, you zag; if he zags, you zig. Each time he turns, either on his own or after you call him, hold out the correct arm and cast him in a new direction. With enough repetition and conditioning, Pup will easily cast in any direction you need."

You'll find that when you begin these lessons, you'll really need to emphasize the proper direction you want the dog to hunt by walking in that direction. Eventually, the zigzag pattern you walk across a field will become tighter and tighter until you can walk a straight line down the middle of the field, only holding your arm out to indicate the proper direction, and the dog will cover it from one end to the other. Eventually, you won't even have to use the signals.

"Try spicing up the field with a few birds, either fresh killed or live flyers," Jurney suggests when asked about an unenthusiastic upland retriever. "Hopefully this will jolt Pup's interest into warp speed and excite him. Spread the birds out on both sides of the field to encourage Pup to hunt the sides. Walk down the middle while Pup hunts the sides and retrieves the planted birds to you. Make a big fuss over him each time he finds a bird, and then cast him off to hunt again with, 'Hunt 'em up!'"

Sitting Steady. Another important skill for the upland retriever is that of sitting and remaining steady at the flush and shot of a bird, waiting to be

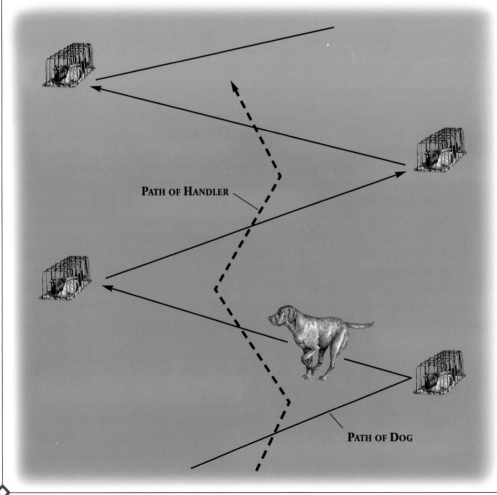

This diagram shows the pattern both the dog and the handler should take in teaching quartering. The birds in the cages at the opposite ends will help to get your dog to go all the way from one side to the other. The path of the handler can eventually straighten out.

PATH OF HANDLER

PATH OF DOG

sent for the retrieve until the hunter gives the command. This is a debatable topic among hunters—both those with retrievers and pointing dogs—and your thoughts on it may depend on the type of bird you're hunting, the cover you hunt, and personal preference. Some say that they want their dog to be right on the bird in case it comes down crippled, so they let the dog break at the flush; others say if the dog remains steady (that is, remains sitting) at the flush and shot, he will mark the fall better, will stay out of harm's way and won't *bump* other birds nearby by chasing one that is flying.

Jurney falls solidly in the camp of requiring a dog to be steady at the flush and shot of a bird. Along with the safety aspect, Jurney says, "Allowing Pup to chase a flushed bird is letting him do as he pleases, and this becomes very self-serving for him. Pup is assuming the alpha role in this scenario."

To train for this skill will take a lot of patience and plenty of repetitions with lots of birds—and a helper or two to handle the birds while you handle the dog. Birds should be planted in a field or in a bird launcher for this exercise. "As the bird flushes, blow your whistle or verbally command, 'Sit!' Pup should be comfortable with this. If he decides to forget his manners, remind him with a tug on the leash while commanding, 'Sit!' or blowing your whistle. Repeat this until Pup will sit on his own without your having to blow your whistle or command, 'Sit.'" Homing pigeons work very well for this training because they provide a reusable stock of birds, but this might be one time when you'll have to bite the bullet and hand over some money.

Shooting. Now that your dog is sitting firmly whenever he sees a bird flush, you can move to the next step, shooting. If the dog sits well on a flush, have your helper shoot the bird. "Only after Pup is sitting [should you] have your helper shoot the bird," Jurney cautions. "Make this point very clear to your assistant: If Pup does not sit, then he is not to shoot.

"After the bird hits the ground," he continues, "command Pup to 'sit' and reinforce that command with a sharp whistle blast. If needed, a tug on the leash will remind him that you are in control and he cannot retrieve until released by you. Avoid sending him as soon as the bird hits the ground because this will encourage Pup to break after only a few repetitions. Have Pup remain seated for a few

seconds one time and an extended time on the next retrieve." If everything goes smoothly, release him for the retrieve with his name, and expect the bird delivered to the "heel" position.

Butch Goodwin said above that self-confidence is the number-one required skill for a fine waterfowl retriever. The same could be said for the upland retriever as well. He will need confidence and drive to tackle the cover and root out birds, and you're trusting him with a lot of responsibility to do this within gun range. Your training will develop those natural traits of intense prey drive and eagerness to explore, and it's never too early to start. With solid adherence to obedience commands, you'll always be able to bring your dog back to your side.

An all-around hunting retriever has to assume roles that are almost opposite each other. As a waterfowl dog, he sits quietly and waits for the command to go retrieve; he comes in at the end of the action. As an upland flusher, he has to do the work first by constantly moving and quartering until he finds and flushes a bird—he has to create the action—at which point you come into the picture. My experience is, given their druthers, most retrievers would rather be flushers because along with running and scenting, they still get to retrieve.

Using Birds. In all retriever work, it pays to occasionally use birds—pigeons, quail or chukars when the dog is small; pheasants and ducks when he's much older and has more experience. All retriever training can be accomplished with bumpers, but a dog that has seen nothing but bumpers during training may go bonkers when he starts mouthing birds on the hunt. All manners may fly out the window, and you'll have a frustrating season on your hands.

So just as you've been incorporating all of your hunting equipment into your training, don't neglect the use of birds. You won't have to use them all the time, of course, but set aside some special drills or special days (preferably when you have a helper available so that you can concentrate on the dog) to work with birds. Particularly if you're having difficulty on blind retrieves, using birds can get your retriever really juiced up to carry long lines, and the scent will really help him to be successful. However, don't force-fetch with a bird. You want to keep everything positive when it comes to working with birds, and force-fetching can be an uncomfortable procedure.

Hunting Season Is Still Training Season

As much as possible, try to simulate actual hunting conditions during training sessions, particularly after the dog has a few seasons under his collar and after advanced skills have been taught and learned–and forgotten. A dog that performs flawlessly in June and July–rock-solid steadiness, expert handling, nailing obedience–can seem to forget everything when guns start going off and birds start flying.

Incorporating duck calls, shotguns, boats, blinds, hunting partners, hunting clothes and birds (pigeons are great training birds) into your training equipment can help settle a dog down for the hunting season. It can also bring to attention problems you may not have otherwise noticed until those first flights on opening day. Training in the off-season for the experienced retriever becomes conditioning to get him in shape, and mock hunting setups reinforce the idea that the same rules still apply.

But when it comes down to it, you won't be able to completely re-create the hunting atmosphere– there is just something about autumn that speaks to these dogs on a genetic level. And that can occasionally erase their memory. For that reason, especially during a dog's first few seasons, you should utilize the hunting months to your advantage and not neglect the training situations they will inevitably present.

That may require that you suspend shooting and leave it to a partner so that you can work the dog; it may also require that you carry along a tie-out stake for a dog that breaks, perhaps a bark collar

for a very vocal dog, or a leash for obedience reminders. Remember that all training aims at accomplishing three things: developing a reliable retriever, recovering the bird and keeping the dog out of danger. It's easy to see how a dog that forgets his lessons can become a safety hazard in and around the boat or blind–or running off chasing deer in the uplands while he ignores a "come" command or a "sit" whistle.

I hunt alone much of a dog's first couple of seasons because I don't want to ruin it for the other hunters; those I go with, I prepare ahead of time for instances that will require us to suspend activities so that I can train the dog. In most cases, I don't even touch my gun and instead focus entirely on the dog's performance. Without the distraction of trying to hit a bird, I'm able to administer corrections at the opportune moment to reinforce the dog's lessons. It is frustrating sometimes to watch my partner shoot duck after duck on his way toward filling his limit, but that feeling is quickly erased when the dog performs perfectly on a long retrieve. And this method also allows me to snap some great pictures I otherwise never would get.

It will take a few years (sometimes more) to get a reliable, comfortable retriever that is a joy to hunt with, the two of you becoming a deadly duo. Don't expect too much during a pup's first season–high expectations lead to too much pressure at the wrong time, which leads to a dog that has a depressed attitude or is cautious to the point of not using his natural abilities and instincts for fear of being punished. Let the dog use his head and figure things out, but learn to recognize the signs when he's in trouble and needs assistance.

That first hunting season or two, you may hunt by yourself a lot so that you can get in some quality training time.

Retrievers will constantly challenge you in your training—even old-timers well into their gray muzzles will present new tests to your patience. Many of these problems can be traced back to training and are not inherent traits of the dog or a manifestation of something haywire in his blood. And many of the solutions to these problems have a common thread—back to basics.

Transitioning from the monotony of simple yard training to the excitement of the field and the hunt can make a lot of dogs go deaf, but you need to maintain your level of expectation in all environments. If the dog is allowed to get away with some things in some places, you'll end up with a dog that misbehaves everywhere.

The following questions address common problems many trainers encounter, whether during the dog's first year of training or after he has many seasons under his belt. You may not care if your dog commits some minor faults when it comes to the overall goal of finding and retrieving the bird or bumper, and that's fine; but just remember that any minor lapses will generally metastasize until they become full-blown problems. The quicker those problems are nipped, the easier it will be to keep them in check.

In the end, however, recognize how excited your retriever is to perform his function, and appreciate that excitement. Sometimes letting the dog get away with a few minor infractions allows him to develop the confidence to use his head and think for himself instead of becoming a full-blooded robot, as Goodwin stated earlier. A true hunting dog knows the rules—and he knows their weak spots, too. The finished retriever will recognize those spots where he might be able to do things his own way to better accomplish the goal, even if it goes against his training; the finished handler will also recognize those spots and allow the dog the opportunity to think for himself.

My dog keeps dropping bumpers—and sometimes even birds—a few feet before getting to me. He might come to the "heel" position, where I want him to deliver, but he'll drop the bumper before doing it.

John and Amy Dahl respond, "The most effective treatment for this is force-fetching. This procedure teaches the dog exactly what you want in the way of pickup, bird handling and delivery. It is also an excellent foundation for further training (multiples and blinds) and a hedge against the development of mouth problems.

"Force-fetching is a challenge for the novice, however, and some choose not to do it. An alternative is to tailor the situation so that your dog is most likely to deliver, practice to establish the habit and gradually work toward the perfect delivery where he sits at your side. When you stand facing the dog, and especially when you ask him to come around to heel, he is most likely to drop the bird. On the other hand, many dogs will fall in beside you holding the bird if you turn your back and walk away. Reach down and, if you can get the bird from his mouth, immediately say, 'Good!' With repetition, if you can get your dog to recognize your hand as a target, you can start receiving the bird facing your dog while backing away, then standing still and finally guiding him gently around to heel position.

"You can improve success on this with many dogs by teaching 'hold,' then using it as a reminder not to drop the dummy. We recommend teaching this gently, with emphasis on success. Otherwise it may backfire. Returning from a retrieve, if the dog anticipates a correction when he hears 'hold,' he is likely to spit the dummy out."

❖ ❖ ❖ ❖ ❖

In training, my dog is very steady—but he goes brain dead during the hunt! In his excitement, he'll break either when the gun goes off or when he sees the bird fall—and I can't correct him because I hunt alone and, heck, I'd like to shoot some birds! How can I cure this? He's flaring some birds and making it dangerous in the blind.

John and Amy Dahl reply, "The sooner you get to work on this, the better chance you have of correcting it. Dogs are experts at discriminating one situation from another and figuring out what behavior works in each. Yours has learned that if he is hunting, breaking gets him to the birds faster, and nobody stops him.

"You're going to have to enforce the rules while hunting, somehow. One possibility is to put a breaking cord on him, attaching his collar to some solid object with a couple of feet of slack. Make sure you are well clear of the tightening cord while shooting! He will learn that he doesn't go anywhere until you send him. As always when trying to overcome a habit, consistency is a must. If breaking is successful some of the time, he'll keep trying it."

❖ ❖ ❖ ❖ ❖

When I'm lining my dog for a retrieve, he scooches on his butt away from my side, and by the time I'm ready to send him, he's about 4 or 5 feet in front of me. How do I get him to stop this creeping behavior?

Evan Graham suggests, "Train him to sit. Many trainers tend to overcomplicate this issue. Creeping is unsteadiness. Unsteadiness violates 'sit.' If you desire to eliminate creeping, uphold the highest standard of 'sit.' There are lots of ways to approach a problem like this. Mine focuses on what I believe is the real issue: obedience.

"It's imperative that you teach your dog all of

what is expected in obeying commands. That's how a dog can understand what standards are. When the rules change all the time, your dog has no reason to adhere to a standard. Keep your messages clear.

"Sitting is not a highly technical skill. It's a basic one. When your dog develops a problem in a basic area, it is best addressed at a basic level. Get him out of the field for a few days of simple obedience—'heel' and 'sit' drills.

"After a day or two of clearing up the 'sit' standard at the most basic level, start carrying a bumper in your pocket. Every third or fourth 'sit,' throw a simple mark. If your dog is rock solid at 'sit,' allow him to retrieve it. If he so much as flinches, or shows you anything except a nice square, solid 'sit,' use your preferred enforcement for 'sit' and deny him the fall. Then walk out and pick up the bumper, and continue your 'heel' and 'sit' drill. Continue this procedure until you get the response that is consistent with the standard you want. Then allow the dog to retrieve.

"This principle should be extended to the field—at all times. In addition, you may find it a useful maintenance practice to routinely deny a mark here and there, to keep your dog from always anticipating [that he'll get to go] just because a mark fell. Keep the standard intact. Keep your dog fundamentally sound, and most other maintenance issues will become smaller and easier to solve."

❖ ❖ ❖ ❖ ❖

I've worked with my dog on various handling drills, and he does great in the yard. In the excitement of the hunt, however, he goes in a different direction about one out of three times—I give him a "back" and he goes "over," like he doesn't trust where I'm sending him. How can I correct this so that he always goes where I send him?

Butch Goodwin comments, "If you mean [how can you correct] on the spot, the only thing you can do is stop him and recast him with lots of influencing movement of your body. If you mean how would you correct it during the next training session, the dog and the handler simply need more time working on 'walking baseball' or the 'T' patterns so that both learn to trust in each other.

"Blind retrieves and casting are a matter of trust. From the dog's standpoint, [it's trust] that there is something there to be retrieved and the handler will guide him to it. From the handler's standpoint, [it's trusting] my dog to run on the lines that I send him on, stop when I blow the whistle and change his mind and his direction when I cast him. There is only one way to develop the trust and that is to repeat and repeat the lining patterns, the casting drills, permanent blinds and some cold blinds."

❖ ❖ ❖ ❖ ❖

Sometimes when I blow the single whistle blast to get my dog to sit at a distance from me, he'll either start to come back to me, or he'll take his time getting his rear end down; sometimes he won't even turn around to look at me. How can I get a reliable remote sit?

According to Butch Goodwin, "All training starts at your side. He must unquestionably sit when he hears the sit whistle at your side. Also, he must be taught the 'look at me' [or the 'here' command, as outlined above] when on the end of a lead so that he looks directly at you at all times. I reinforce whistle sits by using a checkcord looped around a 'snubbing post' (a tree, a fencepost or a stake in the ground) behind the dog. I call him toward me and then at the instant that the cord tightens around the post, I blow the whistle so that the rope stops him in his tracks."

❖ ❖ ❖ ❖ ❖

My dog reacted very poorly to an electronic collar correction I recently gave her, even though it was at a very low level. She quit what she was doing and slunk back to me. I really think I need that control at a distance, but how do I make the corrections not so bad?

Mike Lardy replies, "Your dog is reacting naturally to a correction she does not understand. You can't just slap the collar on your dog and use corrections when she's 'wrong' or 'bad.' You have to introduce your dog to the collar in a deliberate process called collar conditioning. A dog that has not been properly introduced to the collar may think that the correction is coming from the general environment or the spot where she was standing. Bolting away, hiding, refusing to move or slinking back to your side are logical responses for your dog to make to escape the pressure.

"The purpose of collar conditioning is to accustom your dog to electrical reinforcement of known commands, and to have the dog respond to the pressure by swiftly performing the command issued by you. Although you were cautious [in] only using a low-intensity correction, that approach can't make up for the fact that you didn't introduce the collar in a deliberate manner in a controlled environment. The good news is that collar conditioning is a relatively simple process that takes only 6 to 8 days. So get some

good information about collar conditioning and complete [it] before you use the collar again.

"In brief, my conditioning program introduces the dog to corrections on the 'sit' command with the collar gradually taking the place of slight taps with the heeling stick. Later, I use corrections on the 'here' command with the collar taking the place of slight jerks on the lead. When introduced gradually, with known commands, and at a suitable intensity, your dog can learn to respond appropriately to collar corrections."

❖ ❖ ❖ ❖ ❖

My dog is really munching on the birds as he brings them back. How can I prevent this hard-mouthing behavior?

John and Amy Dahl note, "Like many problems in dog training, this needs to be addressed in terms of habit formation. The steps are: (1) stop all opportunities to indulge in bird munching; (2) teach the dog what you desire in the way of bird handling; and (3) practice extensively in controlled settings until proper bird handling is established as habit.

"Force-fetching is an effective method of teaching the dog what you desire. For dogs that continue to mishandle birds after force-fetching, a time-honored technique is to put the bird in the dog's mouth for an extended session of holding practice, with a sharp clip under the chin at any sign of misbehavior.

"Some dogs bite down on birds out of excitement rather than habit. We have found the best course with these dogs is to tailor all of their training to reduce the excitement level and get them acting sensible."

CHAPTER SEVEN

Training Exercises for the Hunting Pointing Dog

Once you get past basic obedience commands, training a pointing dog and training a retriever are very different. Although a retriever will need to know many more commands than a pointing dog will, the former may be practically polished right in the yard or in a small soccer field. Just by going out the front door and using bumpers, you can teach a retriever all he'll need to know about marked and blind retrieves, handling and quartering a field. The bulk of a retriever's work begins at your side. All that's left will be some sessions with real birds or some actual hunting experience to put the shine on and fire up his drive for birds.

But a pointing dog needs those actual hunting experiences in order to learn. Beyond obedience training and a few additional commands and skills you can introduce in the yard, a pointing dog will have to go hunting in order to become a finished dog—he'll need lots of bird contact so that he can sort things out for himself.

The bulk of the pointing dog's work takes place out there, questing the woods or field for game. Consequently, you need to train "out there" in order for him to learn. That's why you may see a retriever in his first season with skills like a pro, but it might take a pointing dog three or four seasons to start firing on all cylinders.

You may need to go much slower with a pointing dog than with a retriever, and you'll need to read your particular dog very carefully to see if he's ready for the next step. A very popular training philosophy for pointing dogs nowadays is that of letting the dog's genetics teach him what he needs to know. If you've been careful to select a pup from a reputable breeder with good hunting lines, you shouldn't need to teach the dog much beyond the basic obedience commands—those that allow you to make him a good citizen around the house and to keep him out of danger in the field. And he'll need to be taught the most important of all pointing dog commands, "whoa."

Then all you have to do is take him hunting, and the birds will be the best teachers of all. He'll learn for himself how close he can get to birds before they flush, how to act around other dogs and how to work cover. You can introduce him to certain things in the yard so that he's a little more prepared in the field, but again, let him figure most of it out for himself when he gets there. This training philosophy is keeping a lot of trainers' blood pressure lower. After all, if the bulk of the pointing dog's work is "out there," then he'll need to do his learning "out there" on his own. With a puppy from sound breeding and bloodlines—and with reliability on the basic obedience commands so that he'll come when called—you should be able to trust those genes; you just need to wake them up.

Concentration is vital—both for hunter and dog.

Skills for the Hunting Pointing Dog

Unlike hunting with retrievers, when a dog could be presented with lots of different situations in which he must make a retrieve, the setting and quarry are usually the only things that vary for pointing dogs. The basic goal is the same—to hunt out in front, locate game and point it until you arrive. But your style of hunting can dictate some of the finer skills that you may or may not require of the pointing dog.

For example, will you be doing most of your hunting alone? If you hunt with a partner who also has a pointing dog, then you may want yours to learn how to *back*, or *honor*, the other dog's point. Backing means that when one dog points a bird, the other dog, upon seeing the first dog on point, basically points the first dog. This is quite a spectacular sight to see; I once hunted with a string of eight Brittanys that backed one another across a vast Montana prairie. The dogs were spread out in a line nearly 300 yards long, and we followed one dog to the other all the way to the one that had pinned the sharp-tailed grouse.

Range is a debatable topic among pointing dog enthusiasts. Where one person may like to have constant eye contact with his dog in gun range, another may allow his dog to hunt all over the countryside, confident in his dog's ability to hold the birds once he has them pointed. The dog can be easily located with a beeper collar. If you're a ruffed grouse and woodcock hunter, you may want your dog closer in the thick woods; pheasant and quail and prairie bird hunters may find it just fine to let their dogs range far and wide because they can see them for miles.

Steadiness to wing, shot and fall is another skill that is up to you. If your pointing dog doesn't retrieve and you have no intention of training him to retrieve, then you may not mind if he breaks at the flush. If he does retrieve, then you may want him to stay solid at the flush and shot and fall of the bird so that he can mark the bird down. If you're a pheasant hunter, you may want the dog right on the bird in case it's crippled, so you may not care if he busts when the bird flushes. If you

only hunt quail, then you'll want your dog to remain still when the birds flush because they often flush low through the cover—here, holding steady is purely a safety precaution to keep your dog out of the line of fire.

Take a good look at the kind of hunting you plan to do, who you plan to go with and where you plan to hunt to see what skills you want your pointing dog to master. The first few seasons will also show you plenty of situations you may not have expected, giving you things to work on in the off-season. That's why it's important to keep a hunting journal so that you can track the skills your dog has down pat, areas where he's lacking, and new skills you want to be sure he knows by the next season.

Getting the Pup Started— Early Points

The most frequent training trick you'll see around pointing dog puppies is the "wing-on-a-string" game. A bird wing or a white handkerchief is tied to a fishing pole and zipped around in front of the young dog, 5 to 8 weeks old. The pup will chase and pounce and try to catch the wing, which is flicked away at the last moment. He'll stalk slower and slower before the pounce, and eventually, heeding some instinct that courses in his blood, he'll freeze and lock up into his first puppy point. All seems right with the world.

Many breeders will say that the pup is a natural pointer—but in truth, this is just a game. If we were to do this exercise long enough with a pet goat, the goat would learn that if he stays still, so does the wing. Sure, it may take the goat longer to slow down and eventually stop than it would take a pointing dog. But that doesn't mean that a Brittany pup that slows and points much quicker than an English setter pup will eventually become the better pointing dog in the field. Still, it's fun to watch a pup start to figure things out so early.

What I find more impressive than the speed at which a dog locks up is the drive and intensity he has in the game of chasing and trying to catch the wing. Pups with lots of drive and intensity and

Those early sight points are something to behold, but they are not an indicator of whether the dog will be a good pointing dog.

desire are much more appealing than the ones that couldn't care less about what's teasing the end of their noses. This high drive to catch prey will ensure that you have an enthusiastic pupil to work with.

So don't be upset if your pup doesn't point the wing on a string immediately. The pup is only sight-pointing right now, and you'll notice him start to point things around the house for no apparent reason—a fly buzzing around, a floating leaf, a shadow. Take heart that the pup is showing how strongly the pointing instinct is coursing through him, and smile at his intense curiosity about the world around him. This curiosity will embolden him, provided you don't do anything to squelch it, and it will help when you introduce him to lots of new people, places and things.

Quartering

While some pointing dog pups will quest a field in search of game as if they are seasoned pros, some may need a little help in developing a pattern of hunting a field that will ensure every bit of cover is scoured. This zigzag pattern is called *quartering*, and you can help steer your dog on this proper pattern right from your initial runs in the field when he's a pup.

You'll first need to teach the dog that his place is in front of you, which shouldn't be too hard with a puppy from good bloodlines. That intensity to hunt and search is right in his genes. I like to encourage my pointing dogs forward with an enthusiastic "Hunt 'em up!" Start using this phrase—or an equivalent of your choice—to let the dog know that it's okay to start running on ahead,

The dog should work the field methodically to be the most efficient, and a good quartering pattern achieves this.

that you'll be right behind. When the pup is really small, always maneuver so that the dog is in front of you; even if he should run past and behind you, turn around so that should the dog look back, he'll see your face. Always follow the dog when starting out, which will encourage his curiosity to explore but maintain his confidence that you'll be nearby.

With the dog trailing a long checkcord, let him run on ahead. Once he hits the boundary of the range you'd like him to hunt (or while you're teaching, the end of the checkcord), give him a whistle and a "come" command to pull him in a bit. When he turns to look at you, start walking in one direction, say to the left and forward, while holding your arm out in that direction. Perhaps give a slight tug-release-tug-release on the checkcord to get him moving that way.

When he reaches the far left, give him another whistle; when he turns back to look at you, start walking to the right and forward, holding your arm out that way. You may need to walk quite a

ways to either side to encourage your dog to turn and start hunting in that direction, but eventually you'll find that your zigzag pattern will tighten. Soon you'll be able to walk straight down the middle of the field, holding your arm out in the direction you want your dog to cast. I like to incorporate a soft, three-note whistle at the point I want my dog to turn, and the spoken command, "This way!" This adds a measure of control that I can use to turn her should we get into heavy cover where she can't see me.

Keep practicing this quartering pattern on your walks and runs, and keep the checkcord on for the time being. You can worry about how the dog is hunting according to wind direction later, when you start planting the field with birds. In fact, the use of birds at opposite ends of the field can help develop this quartering pattern later on, but first you'll want to be sure your dog knows what to do with those birds when he encounters them.

Proper Range

Now is a good time to go into more detail on the question of proper range for your pointing dog. As noted above, this is an instance where personal preference and the type of terrain and birds you hunt come into play.

Some hunters will strap a beeper collar on their dog and turn him loose, letting him hunt far and wide, confident in his ability to hold birds once they are pinned. This method is especially popular on the prairie, where you can see for miles. If the bird has a reputation of holding tight, this isn't a bad option; the beeper collar will go into a different mode when the dog stops, and you can just walk it down until you find the dog.

Those who hunt in thick cover may not like to be out of sight contact with their dog, so they'll want the dog closer. You might hear it argued that hunters who ask their dogs to stay in gun range do so because they don't have the confidence that the dog will hold the birds, so they want to be close enough to take a shot if the bird is bumped. While this certainly is the case with some hunters, others simply like to see their dog work and don't want to have to track the dog down over hill and dale.

I like to see my dog loping through the trees or a field and slam onto a point; it's much more satisfying than just hearing her bell fall silent or her beeper start screaming. Besides, we shouldn't shoot birds the dog has bumped in any case; if we do, we'll end up developing our pointing dog into a flusher.

Again, range is all about personal preference; whatever yours is, you can start developing it when you begin quartering patterns by hitting the dog with a "come" or turn command when he hits the maximum range you want him at. Some breeds or bloodlines within breeds are known to be bigger runners than others, but each dog varies—and any dog will hunt as far as you let him.

Whoa

The "whoa" or "steady" command is the bread-and-butter command of a pointing dog, much as is a remote whistle sit or a "back" for a retriever. Stopping solidly at the word "whoa" or "steady" is the most important skill a pointing dog can learn. (I use "steady" because "whoa" sounds like "no.") It is the one command that all of a pointing dog's work is based on. And just as we refine and reinforce a retriever's natural tendency to fetch things with the force-fetching exercise, so, too, do we refine and reinforce a pointing dog's natural tendency to stop at the scent of birds with a command. This command gives a way to correct a dog that doesn't "whoa," and it allows us to stop the dog when we want to in obedience situations.

Professional pointing dog trainers Rick Smith and Sharon Potter suggest teaching the "whoa" command like a basic obedience command. Begin only after all other basics are finished and the dog responds well to checkcord pressure and trusts your teaching. The dog should also have a nice quartering pattern down.

Smith and Potter teach this command with soft, silent methods that require an even temperament on the part of the trainer. It's pointless to overreact to mistakes or lapses, which will only upset the dog. It's equally pointless to give in to the dog, as he'll then learn how he can get his own way. The Smith and Potter method is one of the most gentle devised, and it helps to build upon our pointing dog's natural desire to stop at scent and encourage his drive and curiosity to hunt.

Whoa Post Setup. In brief, the method uses a setup called the "whoa post," which is nothing more than a stake in the ground. A rope is fixed to the dog's collar, looped around his flank to provide a point of contact and then secured to the post. The result is that when you pull forward on the checkcord or when the dog walks to the end of the whoa rope, the loop tightens

Here's what the whoa post looks like, with a loose loop around it.

The proper setup of the whoa rope is around the dog's flank. This is necessary if you are to get the right kind of pressure.

around the dog's flank, causing discomfort; when the dog stops, the loop loosens. The dog learns to turn the pressure off by standing still.

"The whoa post is not about birds, nor is it to be worked with birds. The whoa post is about one thing and one thing only–it's about standing still," say Smith and Potter. "If you work birds while [the dog's] on the whoa post and [you] have to make corrections, your dog will tie the correction to the birds, and you will create a major training mess."

To get started, you'll need "your regular checkcord, which will attach to the collar as usual; a length of softer rope in a similar diameter and approximately 25 feet long, with a brass bolt snap at one end and a larger loop tied in the other end with a non-slip knot [this will allow the rope to move freely around the post]; and a post that can be easily moved, such as a steel T-post." The non-slip loop is dropped over the post.

Smith and Potter suggest doing a little basic obedience with your dog or even letting him quarter a field or two as a warm-up before moving to the post.

The first step is securing the "whoa rope" to the dog's flank; the trainers are very specific as to how to achieve the proper pressure without hurting the dog.

"Place the snap end of the whoa rope on the ground between the dog's hind legs, then bring it toward you and over the top of the back and down the side away from you. Bring the snap end under the belly and behind the rope draped over the back. You will have a loop going around the flank area, *but never a knot*. Correctly done, this forms a half-hitch. This is important since the half-hitch will release quickly, while a knot will tighten and defeat the purpose.

"Pull the snap end up toward the dog's front legs, keeping it under the chest, and snap it to the same D-ring your checkcord is hooked to. Using the same D-ring will take the action of the checkcord from the neck to the flank as the dog applies pressure. As you work the dog on the post, be sure the rope stays between the hind legs. If you need to replace it, do so, since proper placement is critical in helping your dog understand the stimulation."

Begin the Lesson. Now that you have the dog properly secured around the flank, pressure will be exerted on the flank area when the whoa rope tightens; the dog will learn to turn this pressure off by stopping when the rope tightens, thereby loosening the pressure. Start off by walking the dog at heel with the checkcord and wait for him to stop when he hits the end of the whoa rope. "Drop your checkcord and walk to your dog," say Smith and Potter. "Pick up the dog under the chest and between the hind legs, and drop him lightly from a few inches about 3 feet back. Dropping the dog instead of setting him down helps the dog because he will brace his legs to steady himself as he hits the ground and he is more likely to stand still.... The rope should be quite slack."

They suggest letting the dog stand a couple seconds, and caution that some dogs will immediately walk to the end of the whoa rope again, usually to get near you. If so, just pick up the dog and drop him back in place. Note that you are not saying any command at this point—*you aren't saying anything at all.* You want the dog to learn what the pressure means without throwing in a distracting word that he doesn't know the meaning of yet. Walk the dog in the opposite direction, and repeat the process of letting him tighten the whoa rope, then dropping him back into place where it is slack. You are showing the dog how to turn the pressure off: *Stop when you begin to feel the pressure, and it will turn off; keep fighting it, and it will continue to tighten.*

Here is where Smith and Potter warn that you might have a fight on your hands. "Often a dog will insist on keeping tension on the rope even after several repetitions. If this is occurring, walk to the end of the checkcord and pick it up. Apply steady pulling pressure, gently at first, gradually increasing the level of stimulation until your dog reacts.

"This is where things can get a little wild; the reactions range from what's been called a 'musky roll' or 'alligator roll,' to lying down and refusing to move, to biting at the rope and pitching a major fit. When you [apply pressure], be sure there is no anger involved, and never jerk or yank on the checkcord. Maintain a steady pull, but be prepared for the reaction you will probably see. If you stop at the first sign of trouble, your dog will learn that

the way to stop the stimulation is to pitch a fit, and if you jerk or yank, you won't give the dog the opportunity to turn off the stimulation. Watch your dog's attitude though all of this. During the rolling or biting the rope part, the tail is almost always up, and the dog will show defiance."

Maintain the steady pressure, and eventually your dog will stand up and step back and stand still, slackening the whoa rope enough to turn off the pressure. Drop the dog back a couple paces as you did before, and reapply the stimulation if the dog decides to revert back to his fit.

"It usually takes only a few times before the dog begins anticipating the stimulation," explain Smith and Potter. "[The dog] will stop long before he gets to the end of the rope and even back up a few steps. This is a good sign, as it shows the dog understands how to turn off the stimulation. Continue to work this drill, moving the whoa post to different locations so the dog doesn't learn to respond to just one area. [Dogs] will do this and will act like they are untrained in a different location." Exposure to different settings will show the dog that the same rules apply.

E-Collar. Now is the time to transition from the whoa rope to the electronic collar so that you can have this control while the dog is ranging free. Place the electronic collar around the dog's flank with the probes under the belly. You'll need to walk the dog around on the checkcord and let him romp around with it to get him used to the collar around his flank. "Don't stimulate using the e-collar until the dog is comfortable wearing it," the trainers advise. Do not use the 'hot' button; if the lower levels aren't working, you will need to go back to the whoa post and work more.

"Stimulation on the flank for 'whoa' is a constant stimulation, which is stopped when the dog complies. It is the same as on the whoa post." The work you did on the whoa post communicated the proper way to turn off *any* kind of pressure: stand still. The low levels of the e-collar should now communicate the pressure, and the dog should respond accordingly.

"Once your dog is responding well to the stimulation on the flank, drop the checkcord and walk

The e-collar around the flank is the next step. This dog is getting ready to break...

...but a reminder with the collar reinforces the "whoa"...

...all the way until the handler moves in to flush.

away," instruct Smith and Potter. "Apply stimulation if the dog moves, and also if the dog lies down or sits. You may need to gently lift the checkcord to help with this. Continue this drill over a few weeks until your dog will stay in place, adding some distractions—a Frisbee or tennis ball works well, but anything that would normally cause a dog to move or give chase will do."

Add Verbal Commands. Now you can finally start to say a command. "Once the dog is showing willing compliance [by standing still to turn off the pressure around his flank], give the cue a name: 'Whoa.' Overlay the 'whoa' command with the stimulation, and you will have the ability to stop your dog anywhere. The e-collar gives us the control to stop a dog at a hundred yards while training this command, and it's much easier on both the dog and trainer [than] the old method of having to run to the dog or ride it down on horseback to give it a correction."

It will take many repetitions and lots of patience to get extreme reliability, and only when you have that reliability should you move the e-collar from the flank to around the dog's neck. But you can use the e-collar to mean different things, just as you've used the checkcord (and spoken commands) to mean different things. Smith and Potter explain.

"Stimulation on the neck with the checkcord is applied with a tug, release, tug, release action. When the e-collar on the neck is used for the same purpose [such as for "come"], the stimulation is applied the same way, using either the momentary stimulation programmed into the transmitter or else manually using a tap, release, tap, release on the button. Be sure to try this on yourself so you can tell if the stimulation is actually coming through, since sometimes if you tap too quickly it doesn't register.

"For 'whoa,' the stimulation will be constant, and for 'come,' it will be momentary stimulation. If you are very clear and obvious in the differences both without the e-collar and with the e-collar, the transition is not hard for the dog to learn. If [this method] is not working correctly, go back to basics with the checkcord and whoa post and be sure your cues are consistent before moving back to the e-collar."

Smith and Potter offer a caution about using the

"Whoa" is the most important command for a pointing dog to remember.

spoken command too much or too soon. "The verbal 'whoa' command doesn't come into play at all until the dog has completely learned the stimulation/point of contact. It's easier for the dog to learn this way, since the voice just adds an extra cue that tends to do more to confuse the dog in the beginning. Overlaying the verbal command after the dog has learned the behavior is much easier on the dog."

So in short, just as you communicate to the dog with different spoken commands, just as you communicate to the dog with varying whistle blasts, so can you communicate to the dog through the checkcord and electronic collar. A series of momentary stimulations of pressure mean "come"; continuous pressure means "whoa." And it shouldn't matter where that pressure is applied.

You must have unquestionable reliability with the "whoa" command before you can start refining the pointing process on birds. Your dog will have already shown a tendency to stop at the scent of birds, and he'll have wonderful prey drive and experience hunting afield; now is when you get reliability and confidence in his ability to stop solidly each time he hits scent.

Smith and Potter conclude with some final advice: "The whoa post is where everything finally comes together and you catch a glimpse of the possibilities of the finished product. This is where many people crash in their training. They rush to get to this point, and the dog is not properly prepared, resulting in confusion. If there is any one spot in training where being able to read your dog is critical, this is that spot. Don't be afraid to back off, or go back and rework some of the other steps if your dog isn't handling this part. You cannot make a mistake by going too slow!"

Bringing Birds into the Training Field

There's no way around it—you must use birds to train your pointing dog. If you're lucky, you have access to loads of land and wild birds and can just turn the dog loose and let him figure out the game for himself. But most of us are not that lucky. You'll probably need to bring birds to the dog in a training field or a preserve, or set up some other situation.

Before you start to enforce and teach the steadiness you want, you'll have first been running the dog lots, teaching the quartering pattern and letting the dog experience lots of bird contact, usually set up in launchers. You may have begun to see the dog's natural tendencies take over; maybe he's already stopping at birds when he catches their scent or bumps them. He knows what momentary checkcord and/or e-collar pressure means, and he knows what continuous pressure from the checkcord or e-collar means as well—"whoa."

You won't want to issue verbal commands at this point, but rather show the dog the proper actions and sequence of events.

So with a pigeon, quail or chukar planted in the field, either in a launcher or with the help of a friend to flush the bird, turn the dog loose. He should have the checkcord on, and you might as well have the e-collar on too so that he can get used to it. "Quarter the dog with the checkcord, being careful to not guide the dog to the bird—let him work out the scent on his own, even if he makes mistakes. Experience is the best teacher," explain Smith and Potter. "Be very cognizant of the split second the dog begins to show any sign of catching scent, and gently stop the dog with the cord."

If you work the dog into a crosswind, you'll be able to tell when he catches scent. The wind will blow the scent of the bird out in the shape of a cone, with the bird at the tip of the cone—this is called a *scent cone* (left). When the dog, working forward, hits the scent cone, which will be blowing across in front of him, he will turn

WIND

SCENT IN WIDER AREA BUT WEAKER

SCENT IN SMALLER AREA BUT STRONGER

A bird launcher is a great way to enforce steadiness at the flush.

his head into it. This is the indication that he has picked up scent. Now stop the dog with the cord; he knows that the continuous pressure from the cord means "whoa." "If the dog turns to look back at you, you've tugged too hard. Softer is better, since we want our dog's attention 100 percent on the birds, and we don't want the dog to ever connect a correction with birds," say Smith and Potter.

"As you gently stop your dog, walk quietly up the checkcord and kneel beside the dog. Place one hand under the collar, gripping firmly, and your other arm over the dog's back and under the belly by the flank. Say nothing–no 'whoa,' 'good dog,' etc. Once you're set, launch the bird. Be ready to lift the dog's hindquarters off the ground if it decides to move, which it probably will once it catches on to the game. If the hind legs can't push, the dog can't go anywhere. Expect the dog to stay in place for a minute after the bird flushes." This will help lay a foundation for teaching the dog to remain steady to the flush of the bird, and later, to the shot and fall.

Repeat this drill several times. With the bird in a launcher, you won't have to worry about birds flushing wild and the dog running through them. But what if he starts this behavior after he's had lots of experience and should know better? "Repositioning a dog after a bump and chase equals a correction rather than teaching, and we prefer to train so as to avoid having to do this," say Smith and Potter. "That doesn't mean we never do it, but we will use repositioning to correct a dog that knows better and just made a mistake, rather than to teach." To reposition the dog, take him back to the spot of the flush and drop him from a few inches onto his feet while commanding, "Whoa."

It will take lots of running and lots of birds for the dog to learn the ropes, and you'll need to have lots of patience. You can't go wrong by running the dog and being consistent in your methods of communicating to him; with constant checkcord or e-collar pressure, he should stop reliably, but be ready to apply the same standard all the time. If there appears to be any breakdown, go back to the whoa post where you taught what that pressure means. Begin to incorporate spoken commands once you're sure the dog understands the unspoken communication.

Advanced Skills for the Hunting Pointing Dog

Most of the advanced skills for pointing dogs are polishing touches. While some believe that a dog must possess all of these skills in order to be a complete, finished hunter, a dog that lacks these skills can certainly still be an effective and efficient hunter. Whereas a retriever should be able to handle many advanced skills in order to deal with the myriad situations that may crop up on a difficult fetch, a pointing dog's job is essentially the same, no matter the cover, the terrain or the bird being hunted–search for and point birds, and hold them for the hunter. After you introduce these concepts and commands to the pointing dog, experience and lots of wild bird contact will refine the dog's technique until you have a reliable pointing dog.

Whether you want your dog to master all of the advanced skills is up to you. Remember, though, that these skills will be required should you wish your dog to compete in any kind of sanctioned event. It all depends on what you expect your canine hunting partner to contribute to the hunt, the type of hunting you do and how badly you'd like to see the dog master these skills.

Steady to Flush, Shot and Fall

As noted earlier in this chapter, there are several opinions about how a dog should react after a bird is flushed. Adherents to the quintessential pointing dog theory believe that a truly finished dog will remain steady to the flush of the bird, the shot from the gun and the fall of the bird. At that time, the dog is then given the "fetch" command and is released to retrieve. Supporters of this skill say that it keeps the dog safe; he'll be out of the way of errant shots should the bird flush low. A steady dog won't bump nearby birds while chasing one in flight, and he'll be able to mark the fall of the bird better, thereby increasing the chances of a successful retrieve.

Some want their dogs to be steady only to the flush of the bird. This group usually cites the safety precaution as their reason; they're not concerned about the dog bumping other birds. But they do want the dog to break at the fall of the bird so that he'll get on any cripples as fast as possible. You'll find lots of pheasant hunters in this category.

You'll also find a lot of pheasant hunters—and desert quail hunters—who don't care if their dog breaks at the flush. They don't expect to encounter a safety problem, provided any hunting partners know not to shoot at low birds, and they've lost too many cripples to not want their dogs right on a falling bird. They also argue that training a dog to be steady to wing, shot and fall is a difficult procedure and hard to maintain—and that if you regularly hunt with another pointing dog or retriever that is *not* steady, then your dog will quickly unravel.

As you can see, there are logical arguments for all of these scenarios, and your choice will depend on your personal preference and, particularly, the type of gamebird you hunt. Birds that have a tendency to flee rapidly when crippled may need to be pounced upon soon. Those that flush low through cover may bring a chasing dog into the shooting pattern more easily, increasing the chance that things may go severely wrong.

I've found that most bobwhite quail hunters want their dogs completely broken—that is, steady to wing, shot and fall. Pheasant hunters and desert quail hunters either want their dogs steady at least to the flush, or don't require it. Ruffed grouse, woodcock and prairie bird hunters are a mixed bag; some want their dog to have these skills, while others don't. If your pointing dog doesn't retrieve, then you may not need to worry about making your dog steady to the fall—maybe it's just the flush and shot that matter.

If you do want your dog to master these skills, it will require lots of work and patience and repetitions. You'll need to bring out a bird launcher and enlist a friend or two to help with the control of the bird and gun while you manage the dog. Of course, the dog must be completely reliable on the "whoa" command because that—along with the e-collar around either the neck or the flank—will be how you maintain his steadiness.

Training steadiness is simply a matter of letting your dog find and point the bird, which is planted either in the grass or in a launcher, and then walking ahead and flushing the bird—or having a friend walk in and flush while you stay back with the checkcord. When the bird flushes, give the "whoa" command, perhaps with the continuous e-collar reminder. Work on only one step at a time—first the flush. With many, many repetitions of this procedure, your dog will start to put together the sequence of events; at this point, start phasing out the spoken command—you don't want to have to say it every time a bird flushes while you're hunting and trying to shoot. Gradually phase out the other "whoa" reminders, but be ready to bring them back occasionally to reinforce the behavior you want.

When your dog can stand solidly and watch a bird flap away, start to incorporate a blank pistol into the equation, again reminding with a spoken "whoa" command, the e-collar and the checkcord.

Many pheasant hunters don't mind if their pointing dog breaks at the flush because they want the dog on a downed bird quickly.

Repeat often until the dog is reliably steady to the flush and the shot. If you find your dog starts to break a bit at the flush but then stops again at the shot, the steadiness to flush is not yet completely reliable, so go back a step.

Once you have both steps down, start using a shotgun and have a helper flush and shoot the bird, reminding the dog once again with a spoken "whoa" command and reinforcers to stand still at the fall of the bird. If he breaks at the flush, don't shoot. If the dog is steady to the flush but breaks at the shot, don't let him retrieve or get his mouth on the bird, for that is the true reward of this whole procedure. Only when the dog stays completely steady to the flush, shot and fall of the bird should you release him with his trained "fetch" command to collect the bird and deliver it to you.

I've made this process sound much simpler than it actually is—it can be quite difficult, and you may want to consider taking your pupil to a professional trainer for these skills. A pro trainer will also have access to lots of land, helpers and a steady supply of birds, and he may have easier ways of communicating to your dog what the proper behavior is.

But either way, be sure to participate in your dog's training. Most trainers have no problem with you coming along, and even encourage it—they'll let you flush the bird and shoot it while they control the dog. You can learn a lot in just a few short sessions with a pro, and he'll be able to give you an honest critique of your dog.

If you plan on hunting much of the time with a friend who has a dog that is not steady to wing, shot and fall, your dog may quickly relapse. Take a careful look at whether your dog will really need these skills. At the very least, steadiness to the flush of a bird will be sure to take potentially dangerous situations right out of play. But just as you aren't going to shoot birds that the dog doesn't point, so you shouldn't shoot birds if he busts at the flush. Sticking to this principle will take discipline and may cost you lots of missed opportunities, but it's the only way to show the dog that the standards we set during training apply during hunting.

Backing

If you plan on hunting a lot with another dog, you may want to train your dog to *back* or *honor* the other dog's point. As mentioned above, this means that if one dog points a bird, the second dog will slam into a point upon seeing the first dog, no matter how far away he is. This "honors" the first dog's find of the game, as opposed to running up and "stealing" the point. It really is quite a sight to see two or three dogs lined up through cover, each pointing the one in front.

But (again as mentioned above) if you plan on hunting with a partner and his dog, and that dog doesn't honor, expect your dog's reliability at honoring to diminish once he's had a number of points stolen from him. So take a careful look at who you plan to hunt with; if it's a partner you plan to go with all the time, the two of you can train your dogs together to honor each other. That's doubly helpful because, of course, you will need another dog to train this skill.

That other dog can initially come in the form of a wooden cutout. These dog silhouettes are attached to electronics; they're sold through all of the major dog-training supply catalogs. The cutout dog lies flat on the ground, and when you push a button on the transmitter, the silhouette pops up. The idea is that you work your dog through the field until you get close to the wooden dog; then you hit the button, the wooden dog pops up and you "whoa" your dog when he sees it.

Start off slowly. Have the wooden dog upright, but keep your dog out of sight. Walk him on heel, with his "whoa" reminders in place, around the corner or over a hill; when he sees the wooden dog, give him the "whoa" command. Of course,

This electronic backing dog helps teach a dog to "honor."

he must be reliable on this behavior before you can begin backing training. Either put the wooden dog back down and then release your dog, or release your dog with whatever command you use, such as "okay" or "hunt 'em up." Execute many repetitions with your dog on "heel," reinforcing the "whoa" when he sees the wooden dog. (You can also do this with a real dog, which a helper can put on "whoa" while you are out of sight.)

Now, with the wooden dog lying on the ground, walk your dog toward it, in the "heel" position, using the checkcord. Hit the button, and the wooden dog will pop up; when it does, command, "Whoa." When working with another dog, both dogs should be moving. Your helper puts the lead dog into a "whoa" first; when the lead dog stops, "whoa" your dog to honor him.

That's all there really is to it. You are teaching your dog to sight-point a specific thing—another dog standing still. Lots of repetitions in different environments will convey that this skill must be practiced everywhere. Don't let go of the means to stop your dog should he run right through the honor, and don't rush him too fast through this exercise if you expect sound reliability. If you require the dog to be steady to the flush, shot and fall, you should also require that steadiness when he's the honoring dog. Give him lots of experience seeing events unfold from the honor position before expecting dependability in the field.

When working with another dog, make sure both dogs take equal turns as the lead dog and the honor dog—you want to be sure that neither dog thinks his place is only behind another dog. Each dog must understand that he is to hunt his normal pattern, but when he sees another dog on point, he is also to stop.

Force-Fetch

Consult Chapter 6 on training the hunting retriever for the technique of teaching this skill; the procedure is the same with the pointing dog. However, you may need to heed the warnings that chapter contains even more seriously with a pointing dog. Retrievers have a natural tendency to want to fetch things and bring them to us, yet we still train this behavior to make it more reliable. With many pointing dogs, there is no natural tendency to retrieve, so the process can be very difficult.

Some people may begin and then quit, feeling that the skill isn't that important for their pointing dog to master. Rather, they encourage the dog to "hunt dead," perhaps flash-pointing where a dead bird lies. You may be in this camp, but consider rethinking your position if you hunt a lot of pheasants with a pointing dog. This is one of those cases where you need to look closely at the type of hunting you do in order to determine what skills you want your dog to master. Birds that don't escape very easily when crippled can probably be hunted just fine with a pointing dog that doesn't retrieve; with others, you'll need all the help you can get. I don't feel that there's any reason a pointing dog can't be a non-slip retriever. A dog that retrieves is a better cripple-finder than one that only flash-points downed birds.

Pointing dogs can tend to be softer than retrievers, so you'll have to train the force-fetch with unquestionable patience and level-headedness. But the same principle applies with force-fetch as with the whoa post: Your dog will learn how to turn off pressure by executing the skill you want, in this case accepting and holding a bumper. As stated above, it's best to get lots of advice about this skill from several people, including professionals, as well as a good training video. And as Rick Smith and Sharon Potter stated above, "You cannot make a mistake by going too slow!"

Once you have the "hold" and "fetch" commands down, you can play-retrieve with your pointing dog and start to shoot birds for him. Lots of practice and repetition will polish the retrieve, and you might find that many more birds are added to the bag.

Returning with a fetched bird is the ultimate success. Praise from you is the ultimate reward.

Make hunting fun for you and your partner—and for your dog.

Expectations for Those First Times Afield

You could be one of the lucky ones who picked out just the right pup that learns quickly and seems to know what to do without too much meddling from you. Congratulations; but remember that the boogeyman might still come out every now and then, and you'll think that your dog is suddenly a lost cause.

During the hunting season, there are some things you can do to help speed the lessons the dog will need to teach himself. You might need to keep a checkcord on him for a full season or even two. Dragging it through the woods or field will slow him down just a little bit (don't worry, it won't get tangled too often), and you'll be able to gather him in if he just doesn't want to listen to the "come" command.

It's worth repeating that you should avoid shooting at birds the dog doesn't point. This might mean you have to hunt by yourself a lot if you can't find a hunting partner who can hold off; but shooting at anything the dog bumps will encourage this behavior. If the dog bumps a bird, don't shoot, take him back to the spot of the flush, put him on a "whoa," pet him, tromp around in front and then release him. Shoot only at birds that he points, and quicker than you think, he'll learn that

he can get a mouthful of feathers only when you shoot. And you shoot only when he points.

Let the dog explore the cover and hunt, but also use your ability to handle him to direct him to a thicket or a patch where you have a good feeling some birds might be—or where you just saw one run. If you steer the dog toward the same patches of cover, he'll start to recognize these areas and seek them out on his own to hunt thoroughly.

It really is a different frame of mind you have to have when hunting with a pointing dog versus a retriever. I know—I have both.

My best advice? Don't put too much pressure on your dog or too high an expectation on his performance. Take a good solid look at how much training you did in the off-season and how much "real-world" experience your dog has before setting some goals. I've learned to find a lot of pleasure in different things afield with Allie. Even if I find myself completely frustrated with her performance, I can't help but smile—and feel a little guilty about getting angry—when at night I see her sprawled out, fast asleep, her tail thumping in her dreams from the sheer pleasure of hunting.

Although both types of hunting dogs depend greatly on their bloodline, a retriever can be molded in many more ways than a pointing dog. And there's something about turning a pointing dog loose to hunt way out front in the woods that can be a little unsettling. Will he run away? Will he just keep flushing birds out of range? It takes a lot of trust in your dog to be confident, but that trust only comes over time.

So take your pointing dog hunting or just running in the woods and fields as much as possible. It will be fun to watch him teach himself and learn from the birds. With his set of obedience skills and advanced skills, you'll be able to reinforce the proper lessons at the right moment, and you'll also be able to keep him safe. If he bumps a bird, take him back to the spot of the flush, put him on a "whoa" and tell him what a good boy he is. Let him figure out the cover, and help direct him into thickets and patches where you know there might be birds. Take him to new spots, let him hunt with other dogs, and savor those moments when he locks up like a statue. But most of all, have fun being afield with your dog and watching his utter joy in hunting.

Just as patience in training helps our dog learn quicker, patience in the field will bring results.

I asked professional pointing dog trainers Rick Smith and Sharon Potter to address some of the common problems a person might encounter when training and hunting with a pointing dog. Your dog will always test you and throw new curveballs at you—even after many seasons afield—so this is by no means a comprehensive list. The best you can do is to go back to your training sources and talk to other people who have gone through similar experiences.

✧ ✧ ✧ ✧ ✧

My dog just does not seem to want to point. We worked on "whoa" in the yard, and he seemed to have it down fine, but it seems like the excitement of the hunt makes him go brain dead. He just charges through the cover. He may stop for a couple seconds, but as soon as he sees me approaching, he busts in and flushes the bird!

"Take the yard work to various locations. Often, a dog relates its behavior to its location, and what it will do in one place it may seem to forget altogether in another. This constant changing of locations is called 'proofing' your dog. Once you can do all the basics anytime, anywhere, without birds to distract, move on to using some planted birds and a checkcord. You can also add distractions on the whoa post like a tossed hat, a Frisbee, etc. But never use birds on the whoa post!

"The excitement of a real hunt can really get to a dog, so try to run 'dry' a few times before getting back to actual hunting. This means to find a field where you know there are objectives but no birds and let your dog work it. When the dog handles the dry work, you can try hunting again. One other very important thing: Never shoot at a bird your dog has busted. If your dog doesn't stay steady on point, let the bird go. To do otherwise rewards the bad behavior."

✧ ✧ ✧ ✧ ✧

When hunting in the woods of northern Wisconsin for ruffed grouse and woodcock, my dog seems to want to go off to the side and then hunt in a line with me instead of out front. How do I get her to stay in front of me?

"First of all, be sure you're not walking on a path. The dog knows the birds are in the cover, so the dog will tend to stay in the cover on one side of the trail. Get into the thick cover. If that's what you've been doing and the dog is still off to your side, try this:

"Use a checkcord, and imagine the face of a clock. You want your dog to stay between 10 and 2. Every time your dog crosses either of those lines, change direction and go the opposite way. As you do this, flip the checkcord over the dog's back to cue it to change direction. Don't pull steadily on the checkcord; instead, use a tug, release, tug, release motion. Make sure all turns are out and away from you, and correct the dog if it turns back toward you.

"After enough repetitions, your dog will begin turning by reading your body language, and the checkcord will be superfluous. If you want, you can overlay the cue on the neck using an e-collar and momentary stimulation to resemble the feel of the checkcord's tug-release. The e-collar will become your checkcord when hunting, and after enough time has passed, you'll find yourself using it less and less as your dog clues in to your body language."

❖ ❖ ❖ ❖

My pointing dog responds to all of his commands and whistles very well while dragging the checkcord, but as soon as I take it off, he doesn't listen at all. Any advice?

"The dog is paying more attention to the checkcord than to you. The dog knows the checkcord means business and respects that. And the dog also knows when it is off. Don't let the checkcord drag when you're using it; instead, keep it in your hand so the extra weight won't be as obvious to your dog. We would consider adding an e-collar, using it with the checkcord at first so the cues can be overlaid; then take the checkcord off and use the collar just like you would the checkcord. Your dog will probably become collar wise, but if you're just hunting and not competing, collar wise can be a good thing. Call it added insurance. Your dog will be less likely to rely on the collar cues if you have really worked on the basics. Stick with the lowest possible stimulation level once you start using the e-collar."

❖ ❖ ❖ ❖

Sometimes my dog wags her tail when she's on point. Why does she do this?

"This is called flagging, and is usually caused by uncertainty or too much pressure. There is a small possibility that it could be genetic. If a dog had a bird and the bird started moving or the dog lost scent, the dog's tail would probably start

to tick a bit, and some of the intensity would disappear. This is uncertainty. On the other hand, too much pressure is man-made. Too much correcting around birds, too much hollering, whistle blowing and general confusion in training create a pressure situation that takes some of the confidence out of the dog. The tail is a barometer of the dog's emotions, and it can be used in many ways to 'talk' to us."

❖ ❖ ❖ ❖

My hunting partner told me the other day that it looked like my 3-year-old pointer was "hunting for himself instead of for us." How do I get my dog to hunt for the people instead of himself?

"This dog needs to accept the person as its pack leader. Dogs will respect a strong leader and work with them, but they will ignore a less confident or knowledgeable leader and instead hunt for themselves. Being a good leader means taking the time to thoroughly train the dog before going to the field, and being consistent and fair in your expectations. You will need to allow the dog to learn via its mistakes, and you must show no emotion during training so the dog will accept you as fair and rational. Other than this, follow a training program from start to finish, and your dog will work for you."

❖ ❖ ❖ ❖

We've hunted shooting preserves a lot for pheasants and quail. What can I expect when I start working my dog on wild birds—grouse, quail and pheasants?

"Wild birds are a whole new adventure for your dog. Wild pheasants run more, especially later in the hunting season, and it will take your dog some time to learn how to effectively hunt them. Wild quail tend to fly hard, fast and longer distances than released birds will, and are also more likely to move. Grouse are an entity unto themselves, since there are no pen-raised birds to train on. A good grouse dog will really learn to use its nose, since grouse do not hold well at all, and will flush with little or no provocation.

"In other words, wild birds will be a lot more exciting to your dog, and you'll need to prepare to handle that. It's always a good idea to follow the same routine on the first few hunts that you would at home while training, going from the chain to the lead, and maybe even to the checkcord if you need to, just so you've got a bit of a handle on the dog before you cut loose to hunt wild birds."

CHAPTER EIGHT

Leading Two Lives: What's a Dog to Do?

For the hunting dog that spends 75 percent of the year as a couch potato, hunting season can be seen as a grand vacation, a time to run with the wind, answering only to those segments of the genetic code that quietly urge him to find the game and make the kill. *What's that? Is someone screaming a command at me? Yeah, right!*

At least, those are the thoughts of the hunting dog that's spoiled in the off-season, the dog whose training lapses. While there are few things as satisfying as spending quality time afield and at home with a cherished canine companion, the quality of that time afield is much sweeter if the dog doesn't behave like a blockhead that has seemingly forgotten everything he was taught.

Thus, the dual-life dilemma of a hunting and family dog: Will the family ruin the training by not enforcing commands and asking the dog to do simple things precisely like you do? Will these lapses cause sloppy behavior in the field, leading to a dog that runs through a pheasant slough with his mouth hanging open like he's chasing a tennis ball, without a care in the world for birds or the hunter who may be following him? Must the entire family read this training book so that everybody is on the same page and treats the dog in exactly the same manner?

Well, yes and no. And which questions get a "yes" or a "no" will depend on whether you are a careful observer, set a few ground rules and employ a few tricks the dog will pick up on as cues to what time it is. Dogs are smart, and they will be able to tell the difference between family time and hunting/training time without a problem—but it's also possible for things to get out of control.

Who's Giving the Orders Here?

For the most part, a dog has a tendency to ignore a command given by a person who wasn't very involved in the training of that command. If you have a spouse or a significant other who will handle the dog around the house a lot, it's important that both of you be involved with the training of the dog. But don't train together; rather, you should each spend time training the dog separately, making sure to employ the same corrections, give the same kind of praise and expect the same kind of precision. You can train the dog together at more advanced stages; but for basic obedience, it's best if you each work one-on-one with the dog at separate times.

There is something about the male voice that seems to get a better response out of a dog, so a woman may need to lower her voice a bit in order to open the dog's ears. This isn't sexist, it's just the way dogs react. Often, discipline isn't administered in exactly the same way by men and women, and the dog may remember the correction from a male a little better than from a female.

A riding crop of the kind used by horseback riders is an effective tool for teaching commands such as "sit" or "heel." My dad used it on my parents' two Labs, and they listened well to him, but not to my mom. She couldn't get them to do anything, no matter how firmly she commanded, ordered, pleaded or begged. So she put the riding crop by the door, where she could easily take it out to remind the dogs with a swift crack on the rump

He's a family dog and a hunting dog—but are the expectations the same?

that when she said, "Come," they were to listen. After two instances where a swat was necessary, she came home from work one afternoon to find that the dogs had dragged the crop off the table by the door—and shredded it. They knew that she couldn't back up her words as well as my dad, so they ignored her; but being "Smith" dogs, they were also bully enough that when she suddenly was able to back up her words, they swiped her tool and destroyed it. The latter tendency isn't so common.

Dogs will probably always ignore young children who yell to "sit" or "stay" or "speak" or "roll over." Kids don't have an adult's commanding voice; they don't say commands with the same inflection or emphasis an adult trainer uses during the dog's formal training.

It's a small leap from a dog ignoring a person giving a command to ignoring the command itself. It can be a chore to go through refresher after refresher when you want to do some specialized training—it gets real old, real fast to have to do "sit," "stay," "come" and "heel" with a retriever before you can get the dog to understand that it is time to start working on a difficult blind retrieve. A pointing dog that hasn't been expected to come when called in the house is a disaster waiting to happen. You may end up turning him loose in the field, thinking everything is fine, only to see him streak for the horizon. He never had to come the past few months—well, not unless he wanted to; why should he have to now? Failure to enforce commands around the house can lead to breakdowns in the field that can cost you valuable training time or even birds. If several people in the home will be giving the dog commands, make sure they all know the proper way to give and enforce them and praise for correct behavior.

Playtime Versus Training Time

The dual life of the family/hunting dog can be very easy to deal with if the dog recognizes that he does, in fact, have two separate duties: He is to be a dedicated, fun family member and an efficient hunting partner. While these roles can and do build upon

each other, the training for each should also be significant enough as to be separate and distinct. In the same way, the dog's training should be separate and distinct from his fun time as a family member. There's recess, and then there's going to school; there's playtime and training time.

Dogs have a way of learning schedules by way of external cues, mainly our actions. Or perhaps they fixate on a particular object, an object that's followed by the same sequence of events every time they see it. This process is no different from learning a command. My dogs know every time they see me come home from work that after I change my clothes, they'll get to spend the next 5 or 10 minutes romping in the backyard—one explores the woods, and another maniacally fetches the bumper I toss.

They used to expect to go every single day until they learned through repetition that when it was raining outside, we never went. So now, if it's nice

Using a toy for play fetches as opposed to a training bumper can show the dog that it's playtime—and that he can get away with some indiscretions.

outside at 5:00, rest assured that they'll be waiting for me with perked ears, not letting a sliver of light between their trembling bodies and my legs until I take them out. If it's raining, they simply roll over on the bed and open one weary eye to say, "Hi."

But nothing gets their blood pumping like seeing their electronic collars come out. Then it's business, and they know it. The collars are a sign they understand to mean that we're not goofing around anymore—playtime is over, and training time has begun. Their manners are better, fewer corrections are needed, and their ears are more opened; they remain in better contact with me and my movements, too. Perhaps it's because they know that they can be corrected more easily for misbehavior—they're "collar wise," as some people call it. But being collar wise doesn't account for how they go bonkers when they see me pull the collars out of the bag. Only two things happen when they see the collars—we're either going hunting or we're training for hunting.

It's a good idea to keep some training items solely for hunting training. During free time or family training, use something else. Maybe the item is a particular whistle around your neck, or, as I mentioned above, a certain collar—electronic, pinch, leather, doesn't matter—or maybe it's a shirt you wear that, to them, smells of hunting and being outside. A particular hat drives my dad's Labrador nuts because that's his training hat. If you have a retriever, then use only specific bumpers when doing serious training for hunting, and designate something else for fun fetches; for pointing dogs, perhaps only put a bell on the dog while hunting or training, or maybe he gets a protective vest when it's time to hit the field.

The point is, specific equipment that is used only for hunting or training for hunting can help the dog learn his different roles. A seeing-eye dog, for example, knows that when he's not wearing his harness, he's "off-duty"; off-duty service dogs can be delinquents just like those that haven't had service training. But buckle on the harness, and it's work time. A hunting dog can have his work uniform, too.

Avoid using a particular place to signify when serious training is afoot—you want the dog to mind and be effective in lots of different environments. And that goes for both family manners and hunting skills. So you shouldn't do all of the serious training in the backyard or in the same section of woods, allowing the dog to be lax in every other place, or the dog will begin to associate good behavior with only that particular area—dogs are very place-specific. Besides, a dog must be able to perform any and all commands in several locations, amid lots of different distractions, in order to be reliable.

This doesn't mean that while he's a family dog he should be allowed to get away with blue murder. All playtime should be supervised, and your dog still should follow his basic obedience commands; but it's nice to be able to let the dog be a dog, too, and it's vital to let the family have fun time with him. Specific external cues for the dog to remember and to associate with training will focus his attention to the task at hand and mark a clear line between his two roles.

When it's training time, it's all business. An e-collar, whistle, even a particular hat will help cue the dog into this.

Do you think the dog is going to listen if the child says "Give!"?

What the Family Should Avoid with the Hunting Dog

The separation between family dog and hunting dog can begin to be blurred if the family continues to ask the dog to do hunting-related commands or skills without the proper expectation of performance. And some habits can be hard to break; though your dog may immediately improve when you start serious training, it may take a bit to get him back up to par before you can start working on new skills.

There are some things the family should avoid with a dog that is destined for the life of a hunter; the earlier you set these ground rules, the better. One of the most important is to avoid playing tug-of-war at all costs. This is pretty obvious—you don't want to get into a pulling match with a duck or pheasant. Though some dogs make the switch just fine between a sock and a bird, it is simply not worth the risk. Just never start in the first place. In that regard, there should also be no roughhousing around the mouth or head area at all; you don't want your dog to develop hard mouth habits or fear your hands being around or inside his mouth.

Don't sneak up and startle the dog–this can wreck a dog's confidence and may contribute to the development of gunshyness, especially if the dog is scared by loud noises while playing. All loud noises should be tied to exciting and fun activities to encourage the dog and build up his confidence. Scaring will only make the dog timid.

Excessive use of commands with no consistent expectation of precise performance can lead to a dog that, as mentioned before, first ignores the person giving the command and then ignores the command altogether. If the dog learns that he won't be corrected or enforced until the twentieth time he hears the command, then it will take about that long to get him to perform the skill. This is an especially sensitive area where children are concerned, because they will naturally want to give the dog orders to follow–it's fun for them to tell the family setter to "whoa," and watch the dog freeze. At least the first few times. After awhile, the dog will most likely roll his eyes at the kid. The

best thing to do with children is to be there with them to give the dog commands when necessary, but also explain to them that all they have to do is play with the dog, that if they want him to do something specific, to come and get you.

If you have a retriever, almost as bad as tug-of-war is "chase," in which the dog gets an object in his mouth and the kids chase him around trying to get it back. If he pulls this in the field with a trophy grouse you want to have mounted, you may want to have a word with the children. Or two.

The greatest thing about our hunting dogs is how much we love them around the house, where they spend most of their lives. But in order to avoid ruining the work we've done in preparing them for their lives afield, there are a few things that everyone in the household should realize and understand. Teaching the dog to recognize distinct training times and playtimes–and allowing him to act accordingly in each, yet still maintain his good citizen status–will ensure that he can be enjoyed by all throughout his entire life.

Be sure to enjoy the dog in both training and play situations. And let him enjoy them both, too.

CHAPTER NINE

Keeping Your Hunting Dog Healthy

Like any professional athlete, your dog needs to be in peak physical condition to stand up to the rigors of hunting. Some waterfowl dogs spend most of their time sitting and waiting, but when they are called into action it can be through demanding conditions and terrain; tip-top shape will be necessary. Upland dogs, especially pointing dogs, need the stamina of a marathoner to hunt more than 40 minutes or so. While the hunter may be walking in a straight line, the dog is quartering back and forth in front and will cover many, many more miles. And he's not in comfortable hunting boots.

How healthy you keep your dog–and therefore, an important factor in determining how valuable a hunting partner he'll become–depends on several things: nutrition, preventative medicine and conditioning, and proper first aid in times of injury or emergency. It pays to do lots of research on canine health in order to provide a long, happy life for your buddy. In all cases, remember that a trusted veterinarian is educated and trained in canine health–and he or she knows your dog's medical history better than anyone. You should defer to your vet's professional advice.

Feeding and Nutrition

In addition to the quality of his training, a dog's performance in the field depends to a great extent on his physical condition and nutrition. A dog that tires after 20 minutes is not going to do you much good, nor is the dog that is overweight to the point of causing health problems. It pays to become a label reader: There are numerous brands of dog food–some good, some atrocious–and

different formulas for the different stages of your dog's life. When in doubt, consult with your veterinarian about the proper ingredients and proportions your dog should be consuming in order to maintain his active lifestyle.

The subject of dog food could be an entire book in itself. Still, there are some basic guidelines and things to keep in mind as you choose a dog food. The two most important ingredients that most people talk about are protein and fat. Generally, for active dogs, look for foods with protein content in the 25- to 30-percent range; for fat (the desired energy source for hunting dogs), look for a food that has a crude fat content in the 15- to 25-percent range. A sound meat product listed at the top of the ingredients–or better yet, several sources of meat, such as beef, chicken, lamb, etc.– will boost the essential ingredients to provide your dog with the energy he needs.

Dr. Jill Hyland Ayres and Dr. Rose Davidson, veterinarians in Brookings, South Dakota, provide several guidelines to follow when selecting your dog's food: "(1) To a certain extent, you get what you pay for; (2) companies that focus their efforts on producing quality pet foods generally do the best job; (3) diets that consist of a steady stream of table scraps lead to not only obesity but also nutritional deficiencies; (4) with the current labeling requirements, comparing pet foods based on the label alone is difficult; (5) your veterinarian, who has knowledge of your [dog's] age, health and physical condition, is the best person to assist you in the selection of a pet food; (6) no one dog food is the best food for every dog; and (7) your dog's nutritional needs will change over [his or] her lifetime."

Dogs don't live nearly long enough as it is. Be mindful of all health issues to get the most out of their years.

You'll be able to tell if the dog food isn't very digestible for your dog–you'll have a lot to clean up in the yard. You want to see firm stools, not soft ones numerous times a day. Another thing that can lead to stomach upset or soft stools and frequent bowel movements is changing brands or formulas. If you do this, try to make the switch over the course of a week or two–start gradually mixing in the new food as you decrease the old, eventually making the complete switch to the new brand.

When you decide on a brand, follow the feeding schedule on the bag, and don't just wing it. Some dogs will always be hungry; Labrador retrievers are some of the biggest offenders–they never seem satisfied! You need to control your dog's feeding by following a strict schedule and sticking to the feeding size guidelines found on the package. Feed each morning and evening, when you eat your breakfast and dinner; for puppies, feed three meals a day. In general, I like to go a little on the lighter side of the recommended serving, knowing that I'll make up those calories with dog biscuits throughout the day. Remember that the recommended serving size on the package is the daily feeding amount, not the amount to be fed at each meal.

It's a good idea to limit activity before and after feeding; if you've just been training or hunting, let the dog calm down before putting his dinner down. The problem of gastric bloat (a turned stomach) has been linked to running very soon after eating, but current research is labeling this idea a myth–some dogs are just prone to this life-threatening condition. Still, to be on the safe side, it's a good idea to keep your dog calm for at least a half-hour to an hour before and after meals.

For some of the sporting breeds, obesity can be a real problem. Sometimes it has nothing to do with the dog's food or a voracious appetite–thyroid problems can be the cause, too. But if a vet rules out the thyroid, you've got a little pig on your hands, and a diet prescribed by the vet is in order.

The best way to deal with an overweight dog is, of course, to not have one to begin with. That's why I like to go a little on the light side of the daily serving size. Carrying more weight up top can accentuate a dog's joint or bone problems and make regular walking or exercise–to say nothing of the demanding work of hunting–more difficult and painful. And it can lead to greater potential for injury.

So how do you know if your dog is overweight? Dr. Kyle Kerstetter, a board-certified small-animal orthopedic surgeon at Michigan Veterinary Specialists and Diplomate of the American College of Veterinary Surgeons–and a diehard hunter with his yellow Lab, Remington–says the following: "To judge if your dog is overweight, the best thing to do is look at your pet, not at the scale. You should be able to see a waist on your dog and easily feel the ribs. If you can see the ribs, then your dog may be too thin." With short-haired pointing dogs, you will definitely be able to see the ribs right below the surface; you just don't want an overly gaunt-looking animal. Looking at your dog from the top, you should see an hourglass shape, and from the side, a deep chest should rise to a tighter belly. Some bags of dog food even have a little drawing of what an underweight, normal and overweight dog looks like.

The world of canine food is an ever-growing, ever-changing subject–and big money is involved. Always be reading, always study labels and always pay attention to your dog's shape.

Feeding table scraps to your dog is not a good idea. But saying "No" to those sad eyes may be a challenge!

Preventative Medicine

As with most things, when it comes to canine health, the best defense is a good offense: Taking aggressive, dedicated steps now to keep your dog healthy can prevent many injuries, illnesses and problems from occurring or getting out of hand. Hunting dogs are hard-charging animals that will get bumps and bruises and aches and pains just like any athlete; but with common sense and an eye toward their physical fitness and well-being, you can stop short a lot of conditions–or at the very least, keep your dog in better shape to deal with problems when they do arise.

What's the best form of preventative medicine? Asking your veterinarian lots of questions and taking an active role in your dog's health, including doing research on the injuries or ailments your dog may encounter while hunting, as well as those that the breed may be prone to (such as allergies, canine hip dysplasia, thyroid problems, etc.). Nothing replaces a concerned and observant owner and veterinarian in keeping dogs healthy.

Vaccinations and Heartworm and Tick Medications. Prevention of most canine diseases and maladies starts with your dog's regular annual exam. The traditional, yearly administration of booster shots and tests is necessary for all sorts of things other than the health of your dog. Getting a city tag for the dog, traveling across international borders, and sometimes camping in parks or staying at motels will require you to show proof of your dog's vaccinations.

Shots begin right after birth, and the breeder usually gives the litter their first few series of "deworming" medications when the pups are 2, 4 and 6 weeks old. Our vet will usually give the last series when the new family member is 8 weeks old; at this time you also should get an overall exam of the pup to fulfill any guarantees from the breeder. You usually can't return a pup for health reasons if he hasn't been checked out by a licensed vet.

A series of "puppy shots" begins right before you pick up the puppy at around 7 or 8 weeks, but it may vary by breeder. The pup will receive early vaccinations against distemper, measles and parainfluenza at around 6 weeks; at 8 weeks, he'll receive another series of puppy shots–his DHPP shot (distemper, hepatitis, parainfluenza and parvovirus). About a month later, he'll get his first rabies shot, which is usually good for only 1 year; about a month later, he'll receive another DHPP vaccination. Every year after that, he'll get a DHPP booster; rabies shots can be administered in either 1-year or 3-year boosters. Other vaccinations to talk about with your veterinarian are bordetella ("kennel cough," which will be required if you plan on boarding your pet), coronavirus, leptospirosis and Lyme disease.

You'll also need to have a heartworm test done at this time, prior to mosquito season (mosquitoes carry the heartworm parasite). This is done through a blood or stool sample; your dog will receive monthly pills or a topical medication to prevent this deadly disease throughout the mosquito season, or year-round in the South. It's also a good time to ask about tick medication–the vet will know of the tick risks in your area, but don't forget about places you may be traveling to. Every spring, get that heartworm test done, and after training or hunting, carefully inspect your dog for ticks. If you have a dark dog, you will need to feel very carefully for ticks, or use a fine comb.

Annual exams by your dog's vet is the best form of preventative medicine.

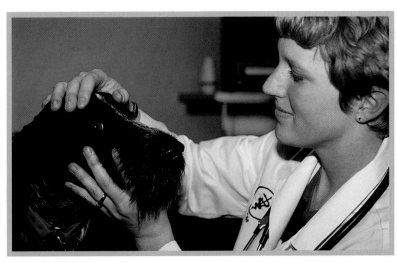

Staying fit is crucial to your dog's success in the field.

Exercise and Conditioning. You don't want to miss a beat come hunting season. Preseason conditioning is absolutely necessary–for both you and the dog–to make the most out of those early hunts. The dog will have a difficult enough time dealing with the heat of the early season; he doesn't need to compound any problems by being out of shape as well. Remember, the dog is much closer than you are to the ground, where air doesn't circulate well–there may be no breeze, and the temperature is several degrees warmer than what you experience. For strictly waterfowl dogs, swimming is a strenuous exercise; dogs can get overheated in water as well as on land, especially in the tepid water of the early hunting season.

Training and hunting present different challenges and obstacles for the dog; that's why I like to do all my preseason conditioning in the actual places I'll be hunting.

Getting the muscles in shape and the heart and lungs worked out will help all phases of a dog's hunting ability and stamina, and he'll be more able to resist injury because he's stronger. But don't push him through arduous summer workouts. Dr. Kerstetter warns against heat exhaustion by saying, "Dogs with heat exhaustion may collapse, have

abnormal mental capabilities, become depressed, vomit, develop muscle tremors or cramps, have rapid breathing and heart rate and pass out. This is a condition that is completely preventable." Carry plenty of water at all times, try to train in the early morning dew or during the cooler evenings, take lots of breaks (of more than just a couple minutes) and recognize when the dog has had enough. Early on, that may be after only 5 or 10 minutes; spend a few training sessions giving the dog a short workout, then gradually increase the time you keep the dog running or swimming and stay at that level for the next week. Then increase it a little more. Careful attention to their workouts will put them in prime shape for opening day.

Grooming. Regular grooming–paying particular attention to the dog's ears, teeth and nails–also helps to keep some diseases and injuries at bay. For dogs with light-colored nails, you should be able to see the quick and keep the nails trimmed short to prevent them being torn while training or hunting. Darker dogs with black nails may require a vet's skill.

Ears should be checked regularly to make sure no foul odor is emanating or extreme wax buildup is occurring, especially after swimming. Your vet can recommend a cleaner that you can squirt in the

Early tooth care can prevent costly cleaning procedures later on.

dog's ears to dry the ear canal, preventing bacteria from forming in the warm, moist environment.

Care for a dog's teeth is a much more involved process that requires vigilance; some veterinarians even go so far as to recommend that we brush our dog's teeth every day. Using canine toothpaste (don't use people toothpaste, as the fluoride and foam can upset the dog's stomach) and a canine toothbrush or finger toothbrush, work the back teeth very well. Certain toys and treats impregnated with plaque- and tartar-fighting enzymes can help,

as do small, medicated pads that can be rubbed on the teeth.

Stay away from canned dog food for your active, energetic hunter—not only are the ingredients not as good as dry food for a dog's energy demands, but the soft meal can contribute to tooth problems. Dry kibble is the best for minimizing plaque and tartar buildup.

All of this—caring for the dog's ears, teeth and nails—is made much easier if you start gently rubbing and handling these areas right when the dog is a pup. Work your fingers slowly and gently over the dog's teeth and gums, and nicely pet your dog's toes. Most dogs will be very ticklish when the fur between their pads is touched, but always be gentle, and try not to have a bad nail-clipping experience.

Travel. As mentioned earlier, the dog should always travel in his crate, and it should be secured in some way (bungee cords work great). Dr. Kerstetter—who as an orthopedic surgeon has seen many dogs come across his table with injuries sustained in car accidents because they were riding loose—is adamant about this common sense, preventative approach.

First-Aid Kit

Just as essential as your gun, shotgun shells, hunting boots and training gear is a first-aid kit—for both you and the dog. Many of its items can be used for both of you, but be sure that your veterinarian

RECOMMENDED ITEMS TO INCLUDE IN A FIELD FIRST-AID KIT:

- roll gauze (3 or 4 inch)
- gauze sponges (3 or 4 inch, sterile if available)
- penlight
- stethoscope
- tweezers (very useful to remove small thorns or ticks)
- hemostat forceps (useful for larger thorns, splinters)
- small blunt-end bandage scissors
- safety pins

- chill pack (commercially available)
- 60-milliliter syringe
- activated charcoal
- antiseptic solution and ointment (Betadine or chlorhexidine)
- unbreakable rectal thermometer
- 3% hydrogen peroxide (used to stimulate vomiting)
- dry mustard (used to stimulate vomiting)

- balance saline solution (1-2 liters)
- eye flush
- milk of magnesia
- vinegar
- lemon juice
- spoon splint
- local anesthetic
- sedative
- medical skin stapler

(from Dr. Kyle K. Kerstetter)

tells you what medications should not be given to a dog (such as ibuprofen). The kit should be restocked every hunting season. Pack a smaller one in a Ziploc bag or other sealable, waterproof pouch for the hunting vest or gear bag that you take in the field; keep a larger one stocked in the truck, and don't forget to pack it when you go training in the off-season.

You can also find already stocked canine first-aid kits through most pet-supply catalogs or stores, or hunting catalogs such as Cabela's, L.L. Bean or Gander Mountain. Though you may need to add to them, they provide a good foundation of materials.

One item that should not be neglected is a canine first-aid book. Though there are several, the pocket-sized book *A Field Guide to Emergency First Aid for Hunting, Working, and Outdoor Dogs* by Dr. Randy Acker fits nicely in a first-aid kit and is thorough.

Finally, toss in some coated, buffered aspirin. This is a great tool for fighting the aches and pains associated with hunting and training; it is also an anti-inflammatory and can help lower a fever. And it can take the edge off of your headaches, too.

Common Injuries and Their Treatment

First off, let me offer some basic, overall first-aid advice: When in doubt, seek a veterinarian's assistance—that's what they get paid for. No hunting trip is worth putting your dog in undue danger, and if an injury looks bad or concerns you, don't listen to the dog that only wants to get back out there. If your dog becomes injured, it's better to put him up and start the recuperation process instead of taking the risk of worsening the injury.

Just as athletes don't get hurt only during games, dogs don't get injured only during hunting season. Training season is just as demanding, and as full of potential for injury, as a hunt.

Putting a bandage or a muzzle on a dog for the first time is much easier if the dog is not injured. So practice your technique in the off-season. It isn't possible to practice all first-aid techniques, but take a look through your first-aid book and rehearse those that you can. You might also use this time to teach

your dog a new command—or greatly reinforce those he already knows, such as "down"—that might help you to calm him or make him be still so that you can administer first aid. When an injury does happen and the dog is in pain, you don't want to bumble your way through a basic first-aid procedure.

This chapter contains a few basic first-aid procedures that you can do very easily, but always talk to your veterinarian. When you make an appointment for your dog's yearly vaccinations, tell the vet that you would also like to take a few moments to discuss field first aid. Ask all the questions you can think of. Nothing replaces the expertise of these professionals; they can show you proper techniques, perhaps prescribe or sell you valuable items for your first-aid kit, and discuss emergencies with you.

Laceration. Hunting dogs will get many cuts and scrapes during the season; the more serious lacerations will require immediate attention but can be cared for in the field. Extreme lacerations, such as the severing of an artery, will require the application of direct pressure, clamps or even a tourniquet. Consult your veterinarian and first-aid book for proper procedures in those extreme cases.

For mild cases, it is important to clean the wound, especially if the cut came from barbed wire (which can be submerged in farm marshes where you may be duck hunting). Use a wound cleaner such as Nolvasan or Betadine, available from your veterinarian or pet-supply store. You'll need to bandage the wound if necessary. If you must apply direct pressure to stop the bleeding, do not remove the bandage once it has soaked through, as you may rip away any clots that are beginning to form. Simply apply a fresh bandage on top and let the vet clean the wound and apply a fresh dressing. If the wound isn't serious, regular application of wound cleaner and antibiotic ointment during the healing process will help. Most cuts are superficial; deeper ones should be treated as emergencies with a rush visit to the vet.

Torn Nail. According to Dr. Randy Acker's book: "Though not an extreme emergency, torn and severely split nails should be removed promptly following the procedures listed below. Most nail injuries heal quickly and the nail will almost always regrow when extracted. Bone infection can result from torn nails, requiring toe amputation.

Symptoms: Frequent licking of toe; nail visibly split.

Field Treatment: Muzzle dog...; trim other unsplit nails; grasp torn nail firmly with hemostat or needlenose pliers and pull off forcefully.

Note: If unable to do this, trim split nail as short as possible. Clean toe with Betadine solution; bandage; [administer] a broad spectrum antibiotic.

Prevention: Keep nails regularly trimmed.

Caution: If nails are trimmed too short, they will bleed, sometimes for hours. Taking small bits off can help you avoid cutting into the quick, and Quick Stop powder or styptic pencil can stop the bleeding."

I've found that the type of nail clippers that are shaped like miniature guillotines produce the quickest, cleanest cuts; make sure to keep an extra set in your first-aid kit. Torn nails are bothersome and can happen anywhere—one of my dogs ripped a nail simply jumping down from the tailgate of the truck, and it hobbled her the rest of the day.

Lameness. It isn't uncommon for a dog to twist an ankle or elbow while hunting, and dogs are usually pretty stiff the evening after the hunt. Coated, buffered aspirin can help them deal with some of these aches and pains.

But don't trifle with lameness in the field. Stop hunting and give your dog a spot inspection, trying to locate the source of the injury. It may be that he stepped in a hole wrong and just tweaked a paw; or he could have torn a tendon or blown out a knee. In any case, take it easy on the dog—remember how far he's running compared with how far you're walking. If you have to quit, quit—it's much more important to let your dog recuperate than to keep hunting and risk worsening an injury. Some dogs don't know how to tone down their drive; they can be their own worst enemies, so it's up to you to recognize when they are in pain and need to be told to stop. Remember, you can always hunt again the next day.

Bandage and Splint Application. If you see that the dog has a sprain or a broken bone, or if there is severe bleeding, you'll need to apply a bandage and perhaps a splint, depending on the injury. "A bandage offers immobilization of the limb or support and protection for underlying wounds," Dr. Kerstetter explains. "A bandage consists of three

layers: The first layer is the contact layer and is applied directly to a wound. This can be gauze or a non-adherent dressing such as Telfa or Adaptic. The second layer is usually cotton wrap and will absorb any fluids from an underlying wound. If no wound is present, the middle layer acts solely to immobilize the limb. The outer layer serves to support and protect the underlying layers. It can be made of bandage tape such as Vetwrap or Conform tape. Adhesive tapes such as white athletic tape or Elasticon may also be used, and in a pinch duct tape works great.

"It is extremely important to not apply the bandage so tight that it cuts off circulation. If the toes begin to swell, turn blue, or are cold, the bandage is too tight and must be removed immediately."

For splint application, "If a lower limb or foot has suffered a fracture, a temporary splint should be applied. The simplest method makes use of a spoon splint or metasplint that is commercially available. Apply the splint on the back of the limb between the second and third layer of a bandage. If a commercial

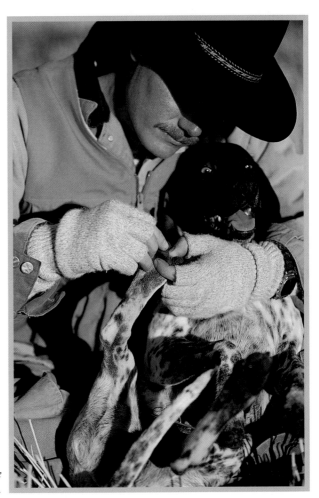

Injuries to the foot or leg are the most common for hunting dogs.

splint is not available, use a rolled up newspaper or card board to fashion a splint. Seek veterinary attention immediately."

Porcupine Quills. All pointing dogs and retrievers will probably come in contact with a porcupine at some point, and it usually takes only one encounter to train them—a face full of quills tends to be a good teacher. The porcupine does not, of course, shoot out the quills at the attacking dog; rather, the dog sticks himself when he attacks the rodent. If the dog stands back and barks, he won't get quilled; when he tries to bite—or fetch—the trouble begins.

That's why I always carry a pair of needlenose pliers on my belt. Dr. Acker's book says "If the dog has only a few quills penetrating the skin, these can generally be removed by holding down surrounding skin and grasping the quill near the skin with a hemostat or needlenose pliers and pulling firmly. Try not to break the quills off, as they are difficult to locate under the skin. Note: When you pull the quill, the surrounding skin will come toward you; thus it is necessary to hold the skin close to the body to prevent nearby quills from slipping under the skin.

"If the dog has a great many quills, especially in the mouth and head area, or if the dog is resisting and breaking quills off, anesthesia may be required to remove them. See [your] vet. Be prepared for your dog to be in a foul mood and even bite you as you try to help him out. Just do your best to calm the dog, and work quickly but thoroughly.

"Caution: Do not pull a quill that has gone clean through the cornea. As quills can migrate under the skin and cause other complications, they should be removed promptly. However, it is okay to wait 24 to 48 hours before removing quills if you are in an unusual situation. Note: It is not effective to cut the tip of the quills off or soak quills in vinegar." His book also says that a tranquilizer, which you can probably obtain from your vet, can help to calm the dog so the quills can be removed.

Snakebite. If you're in the western states, chances are pretty good that you'll come across a rattlesnake at some point. Ask your veterinarian about a snakebite kit you can take in your vest; the vet may even be able to provide you with some of the supplies you'll need. In the event of a snakebite, quit hunting and get to a vet immediately. If you hunt in snake country all the time, your vet may be able to recommend a "snake-breaking" training class or seminar.

Hypoglycemia. On the first-ever hunt with one of my pups, we all overdid it in the South Dakota heat. And in her excitement, she wouldn't eat any-thing—either in the morning or as a snack out in the field. About 2 hours into the hunt, she started to slow down dramatically, and her breathing became very labored. I called her to heel and grabbed her checkcord, guiding her to lie down in the shade and take some water. She slurped a little,

Though you might be able to remove most of the quills yourself, always have the dog seen by a vet as soon as you can.

and then her vigorous panting began to slow, too; she climbed to wobbly feet and started ambling off sideways. That's when I forced her to the ground and poured more water in her mouth. Then she stopped panting altogether. I carried her about 2 miles to the truck.

We forced her to drink lots of water, and I shoved a peanut-butter-and-jelly sandwich down her throat, smearing the jam on her gums and tongue. A close friend we were hunting with brought out an energy paste and rubbed it on her gums, and her eyes started to sparkle again. In no time, she was on her feet and drinking—and begging for more sandwiches—on her own. Later that afternoon, she went on to hunt for another hour.

"This is sometimes called 'hunting dog collapse,'" Dr. Kerstetter says. (She probably also had a touch of heat exhaustion.) "Hypoglycemia is [a decrease to] low levels of blood glucose and is sometimes observed in dogs at the beginning of the season. This can result in weakness, collapse and seizures and is primarily the result of poor conditioning and poor nutrition. [It] can be prevented by feeding your dog appropriate rations for 1 to 3 weeks before conditioning, and conditioning for at least 3 weeks before hunting."

Some dogs are prone to hypoglycemia, while others have tremendous endurance and stamina on an empty stomach. Drs. Ayres and Davidson recommend carrying a peanut-butter-and-honey sandwich as a snack for dogs in the field. Proper conditioning and a balanced diet fed throughout the year will provide the necessary energy requirements for your dog so that you won't have to carry him out of the field.

Eye Washing. Upland dogs can get lots of grass seeds and awns in their eyes as they tear through the cover, and after the hunt, you may see them squinting a lot; perhaps there will be some discharge as well. Carefully open the dog's eyes wide and pull the lid down a bit; you may see a mess of stuff lodged there. With a saline solution in hand, hold the dog's muzzle up, keep the eye open and drop the eye flush in. The dog should blink the foreign matter right out, or at least to a position where you can wipe it away.

If the situation looks more severe—like something has cut, scratched or penetrated the eyeball—close the dog's eye, put a gauze patch over it and get to the vet.

Household Dangers

As the title of this book indicates—and as I've mentioned time and again—our dogs are family members, too. But the house can be a pretty dangerous place for an animal. Just as we "baby-proof" our home for a child, we should also "dog-proof" it. We need to recognize the dangers that lurk in the house and get them out of canine reach.

Chocolate can be deadly to dogs. It naturally contains theobromine, which is toxic to dogs in certain amounts. Baking chocolate seems to be more dangerous than milk chocolate, but it's best to remove all types. You'll need to watch carefully during the holiday season—especially if you have kids who hold everything right at dog-eye level.

Automobile antifreeze should be kept away from your dog at all costs. The ethylene glycol in the liquid causes poisoning. A dog that is suffering from antifreeze toxicity will require drastic and immediate medical attention. Another type of poisoning I am unfortunately all too familiar with is one involving bait put out to control mice or rats.

"The best-case scenario is when the pet is observed to have been in contact with the toxin, and medical attention is sought immediately," Drs. Davidson and Ayres say. "It is always better to be safe than sorry, and a call to your veterinarian right away can prevent the disastrous effects that may result from the toxin exposure."

By no means is this chapter meant to be the end-all discussion for canine health care, nor does it address all the dangers or emergencies that can arise either at home or in the field. Always be reading about this ever-changing subject, and stay current on the latest breakthroughs in canine nutrition and first-aid tools and procedures. Get a well-referenced home veterinary book that is easy to understand and follow, and talk over all the potential dangers you may encounter with your vet and fellow dog owners. Your dog's life is short enough as it is.

Reflections from a Hunting Journal

Kingsley Area, Michigan

Spectacular day down in Kingsley. Beautiful colors, birds and dog work. Took both dogs out by myself and left Josie howling in the truck for the first half-hour.

Allie worked really well, but nothing in the open area along the trail. We moved to the fringes of the young aspen, walking in the pines, and she walked into a point—still panting, but pointing. I told her, "Steady," while I walked up and then just sort of stood there. A woodcock busted out of the other side, and I had to run forward a few steps to see it flying down the treeline—no shot. We got the bird up again later when she bumped it.

After putting Allie up and working Josie for a little while—and scratching down two woodcock—I got Allie back out of the truck with 8 minutes to go until shooting time was over. There were a couple more cover edges I hadn't hit yet.

Back on the edge of the young aspen cut, with about 3 minutes to go until dusk, Allie slammed on point and stayed steady while I walked in front of her to flush—nothing. I released her; she went about 15 steps and pointed again, but cautiously. Again, she remained steady while I walked in front—and still nothing.

About a minute to go, so we walked back toward the truck. She cast to my left, and then whirled around and absolutely nailed a point in a bush on the edge of the young aspens but in the pines. She had her chest down, right leg pulled up, butt high and tail high. I walked over there—nothing! I released her, and she took about 3 steps around the bush and slammed again—now she was facing me. I looked down—and saw the bird! It swished its tail and then flushed. I missed with the right barrel and mumbled, "Oh no!" But I caught up with the left and dropped it—right as shooting time ended. We hurried over to where it fell—and nothing. No bird. I called Allie back over, and she went about 10 paces from where I was looking and flashed a quick point—and then picked up the bird, her first woodcock!

Bryant Slough, South Dakota

What a day! Back to Bryant Slough, only Greg and I set up in the right spot this time. And the ducks—all gadwalls and a few wigeons—kept decoying straight in. Greg got his six birds in 30 minutes, and I shot one, missing a couple more.

So the birds were amazing—still decoying when we were picking up—and the shooting was so-so. Better than yesterday. But the story was Josie.

I handled Josie while Greg shot—that was the deal. With reminders, she stayed on every bird until sent, chasing down a couple cripples and finishing every single retrieve—as she always does—with perfect style at heel. On the bird I shot, she broke and was almost to the bird when I called her back; then

I lined her up properly and sent her back for it.

But it was the blind retrieve today—a 150-yard blind to the middle of the shallow, mucky pothole—that made my season thus far.

A hit bird sailed then crumpled out in the middle, landing in the muck. After we were done hunting, it came time; I lined Josie up and sent her. What Greg and I initially thought was about an 80- to 100-yard retrieve quickly proved longer when Josie got out 40 yards beyond the decoys and was only halfway there. With a couple "backs," a couple "overs," one collar correction and a perfect "angle back" that she took over her left shoulder, she scented then spotted the bird about 20 yards away. She nearly leaped out of the water, scooped it up and walked the entire way back, taking about 5 minutes to get all the way back to shore. I even stopped her halfway back to let her catch her breath! She just calmly walked all the way to shore, came right to heel and sat, holding the bird.

Amazing. Everything we'd trained for. Everything. She took a great line to begin with, getting a little sidetracked with all the duck scent out there, but she stayed the course pretty well, only needing a little handling. She's learned to trust me and to stay on line, knowing she can turn to me for direction. And as today proved, that's at any distance.

Someday Soon

Someday soon, my master, I will hunt for you. My bell will clang through the woods, and when it falls silent, you'll be reminded of the one who has gone before me, the one whose collar and bell I now wear. Someday soon, my master, I will wait for the first flights with you, and the wind and the rain will be harbingers of the ducks and geese. Then, we will work as a finely tuned battery, each wanting to do our best for the other.

Someday soon, my partner, this simple wing that I now point will be an anxious grouse; my long, feathered white tail will be a signal that I have done my job, that it is now time for you to have fun—for that is what I truly crave. Someday soon, my partner, this playful game of fetch will help me to bring back your prized duck so that you may put it on the wall, perhaps next to a picture of you and me.

Someday soon, my friend, these eyes of mine that look at you and say, "I will do my best for you every day of my life," will be weary and gray. Your eyes will be sad as they see me hobble and struggle, but mine will always search for your desires. Maybe I'll flash-point that wing in the corner or put that old bumper in your lap, and we can once again be teacher and student, master and servant, partners. Someday soon, my friend, we will have to say good-bye for a brief time, but I will be waiting for you—on a staunch point under a golden aspen tree, or on the rocks by the pounding surf, scanning the skies for birds.

Someday soon, I will be gone, so enjoy me now; savor these precious weeks that I am a puppy; cherish the memorable years we will hunt together. For someday soon, all you will have to remember me by is that dusty bumper or that weathered collar and bell, and those tender memories that will grow brighter each time you think of me.

Appendix

CONTRIBUTING TRAINERS AND VETERINARIANS

Dr. Jill Hyland Ayres and Dr. Rose Davidson

Graduates of the Iowa State University College of Veterinary Medicine, Dr. Ayres and Dr Davidson opened the Gentle Doctor Animal Hospital in 1996 in Brookings, South Dakota, a strictly small-animal practice. Their practice mission is to provide the highest quality of veterinary medicine and surgery possible in an atmosphere of sincere compassion and concern. They are regular columnists for *Just Labs,* and they are both Labrador retriever owners as well.

John and Amy Dahl

This husband-and-wife team have trained retrievers of all breeds since 1971. John has trained and handled six dogs to their field championships. He and Amy have trained hundreds of personal gun dogs and a number of master hunters. They are regular contributors to *The Retriever Journal* and *Just Labs* magazines, and have been featured in several other dog and sporting magazines. They are coauthors of *The 10-Minute Retriever,* a book on beginning retriever training, and John has written books on gun dogs and gamebird hunting. They can be contacted at www.oakhillkennel.com; or you can write to them at Oak Hill Kennel, P.O. Box 1605, Pinehurst, NC 28370.

Butch Goodwin

Butch Goodwin has had a passion for raising and training Chesapeake Bay retrievers for almost two decades. He is the owner and operator of Northern Flight Retrievers in New Plymouth, Idaho. He is a nationally recognized specialist in the field of retriever gun dog training, and is a columnist for *The Retriever Journal.* In addition, he will soon be offering a comprehensive book on retriever training. For more information, look up his website at www.northernflight.com, or write to Northern Flight Retrievers, 4965 Freemont Road, New Plymouth, ID 83655.

Evan Graham

This retired professional dog trainer and ex-paramedic is also a contributing writer for *The Retriever Journal* and has trained and handled many dogs that earned positions on the National Derby List, including five in a single year, one of them being number three. At least three of the dogs he trained as a professional became field champions. Along with *Smartwork for Retrievers Volume One: Basics and Transition,* now available is

Smartwork II: Secrets of the Pros, which outlines late transition and advanced training. In addition, this second volume of the Smartwork system offers unique information about maintenance and preparation for field trials, hunt tests and hunting the fully trained retriever. Evan can be contacted through Rush Creek Press, P.O. Box 680, Liberty, MO 64069. E-mail at rushcreekpress@aol.com, or check the website at www.rushcreekpress.com.

Charlie Jurney

Charlie Jurney owns and operates Beaverdam Kennels in Terrell, North Carolina. He has been training dogs for approximately 20 years and has earned numerous upper-level titles in United Kennel Club hunt tests, North American Hunting Retriever Association field tests and American Kennel Club hunt tests. After the death of renowned dog trainer Richard Wolters, Jurney was asked to make the video versions of the books *Game Dog, Gun Dog,* and *Water Dog,* which have been best sellers in the video training market. Recently, Charlie completed his own book, *Finished Dog,* which is available in a bound field manual or on a CD-ROM for the computer. He has also been a contributing author for *The Retriever Journal, The Pointing Dog Journal, Just Labs, NAHRA News* and *Waterfowl USA.* You can visit his website at www.finisheddog.com.

James Keldsen

James Keldsen resides in Walkerton, Indiana, with his wife, children and their Labrador retrievers. Working as a health and safety manager, he is also a freelance writer and photographer. He writes the "One on One" column for *The Retriever Journal* and contributes to several other retriever publications, including *Just Labs.* He is actively involved with field retrievers, hunting and running hunt tests. He serves as an officer with the Master National Retriever Club and has served on the board of his local retriever club. He and his wife breed and raise Labrador retrievers under the Pine Acre Retrievers kennel name. You can contact him at 31720 Riley Road, Walkerton, IN 46574; retrievers@pineacre.com; www.pineacre.com.

Dr. Kyle Kerstetter

Dr. Kerstetter received his DVM in 1993 from Ohio State University College of Veterinary Medicine and did an internship at Michigan State University in small-animal medicine and surgery. He currently works at Michigan Veterinary Specialists and achieved his board certification in small-animal surgery in 1999. He enjoys hunting with his Lab, Remington, and training retrievers.

Mike Lardy

Mike Lardy has trained more than 60 field champions and has won the National Retriever Championship a record six times. You can find more of Mike's championship training in *Training with Mike Lardy, Volumes I and II*, compilations of Mike's columns from *The Retriever Journal*. His three comprehensive training videos and manuals—*Total E-collar Conditioning, Total Retriever Training*, and *Total Retriever Marking*—are some of the best around. All are available from Younglove Broadcast Services at (800) 848-5963, or on the Internet at www.totalretriever.com.

Rick Smith and Sharon Potter

Internationally renowned trainer Rick Smith travels the world teaching his highly successful Silent Command System to bird-dog owners of all breeds. Rick has trained and handled five International Open Brittany champions and three National Open Brittany champions; he holds the record for the most U.S. Open Brittany champions with seven wins. Several of these dogs are members of the Field Trial Hall of Fame, including the only Brittany in history to win a 3-hour championship against pointers and setters.

Sharon Potter is an avid hunter and archer and has written for numerous publications on a wide variety of subjects, from horses to bowhunting to dog training. She has been training dogs for pleasure hunting for many years, including hunting retrievers, coonhounds and pointing dogs. Sharon travels with Rick Smith to assist with his bird-dog training seminars whenever her schedule allows.

Rick and Sharon, columnists for *The Pointing Dog Journal*, are about to publish their first book, *Train Your Bird Dog with Rick Smith*, and Rick has the first of a series of training videos available as well. Rick's very popular dog-training seminars focus on teaching owners to train and understand their own bird dogs. For more information, Rick can be contacted at (830) 216-4230, or write to him at 27279 Mathis Road, Pleasanton, TX 78064.

CLUBS AND ORGANIZATIONS

American Birddog Classic Field Trial Club
www.americanbirddogclassic.com

American Kennel Club (AKC)
260 Madison Ave.
New York, NY 10016
(212) 696-8200
www.akc.org

Canine Eye Registration Foundation (CERF)
Purdue University
625 Harrison St.
W. Lafayette, IN 47909-2026
(765) 494-8179
www.vet.purdue.edu/~yshen/cerf.html

American Field Publishing Company
542 S. Dearborn St., Suite 1350
Chicago, IL 60605
(312) 663-9797; fax: (312) 663-5557
www.americanfield.com

Hunting Retriever Club, Inc. (HRC)
P.O. Box 3179
Big Spring, TX 79721-3179
www.hrc-ukc.com

National Bird Hunters Association (NBHA)
www.nbhadog.org

National Shoot to Retrieve Association (NSTRA)
226 N. Mill St. #2
Plainfield, IN 46168
www.nstra.org

North American Gun Dog Association (NAGDA)
13850 C.R. 31
Stratton, CO 80836
(719) 348-5451; fax (719) 348-5999
www.nagdog.com

North American Hunting Retriever Association (NAHRA)
P.O. Box 5159
Fredericksburg, VA 22403
(540) 286-0625; fax (540) 286-0629
www.nahra.org

North American Versatile Hunting Dog Association (NAVHDA)
P.O. Box 520
Arlington Heights, IL 60006
(847) 253-6488; fax (847) 255-5987
www.navhda.org

Orthopedic Foundation for Animals (OFA)
2300 E. Nifong Blvd.
Columbia, MO, 65201-3856
(573) 442-0418; fax: (573) 875-5073
www.offa.org

Pennsylvania Hip Improvement Program (PennHIP)
www.vet.upenn.edu/ResearchCenters/pennhip

Pheasant Hunters Unlimited
995 E. County Rd. 1550
Hamilton, IL 62341
www.phuhunt.com

United Kennel Club (UKC)
100 E. Kilgore Rd.
Kalamazoo, MI 49002-5584
(269) 343-9020; fax (269) 343-7037
www.ukcdogs.com

Index

Contributing Photographers & Illustrators

Denver Bryan
DenverBryan.com
© *Denver Bryan: front cover inset, back cover TR, pp. 3R, 21, 24, 35, 74, 75, 101, 122, 123, 124, 128, 130*

Dembinsky Photo Assoc.
Owosso, MI
© *Daniel Dempster: pp. 15BL, 18L, 26, 40T*

Alan & Sandy Carey
Bozeman, MT
© *Alan & Sandy Carey: pp. 56, 62*

Lon E. Lauber
LonLauber.com
© *Lon E. Lauber: back cover TL, BR, pp. 3L, 6, 15TR, 17BL, 19, 27, 28, 29, 30 both, 31, 33, 34, 36, 37, 39R, 41R, 44R, 45, 48, 50, 52, 55, 57, 58, 59, 60, 61, 70, 72, 73, 77B, 87 both, 88 both, 93, 95, 99, 106, 114, 115, 116, 125*

Bill Marchel
billMARCHEL.com
© *Bill Marchel: pp. 10, 39L, 42B, 42T, 69, 92, 105, 129*

Greg Meader
North Oaks, MN
© *Greg Meader: p. 3C*

Sharon Potter
Woodruff, WI
© *Sharon Potter: pp. 107, 108 both, 110 all*

Mark Raycroft
Trenton, Ontario, Canada
© *Mark Raycroft: p. 17TR*

John Schafer
Harsen's Island, MI
© *John Schafer: pp. 4, 9, 68, 136, 137, 131*

Dusan Smetana
DusanSmetana.com
© *Dusan Smetana: back cover CR, pp. 11, 14, 43R, 66, 102, 118, 133*

Dale C. Spartas
Spartasphoto.com
© *Dale C. Spartas: front cover, pp. 8, 16, 18R, 23, 32, 39C, 40B, 41L, 43L, 44L, 47, 64, 67, 71, 76, 79, 80, 84, 91, 98, 100, 111, 112, 117, 120, 126, 134*

Ron Spomer
Bloomington, IN
© *Ron Spomer: pp. 12, 17BR, 38, 53, 54, 90, 94*

<u>ILLUSTRATOR</u>:

Chris Smith
Interlocken, MI
© *Chris Smith: pp. 77, 78, 81, 82, 96 112*

(Note: T=Top, C=Center, B=Bottom, L=Left, R=Right)

Creative Publishing international is the most complete source of How-To Information for the Outdoorsman

THE COMPLETE HUNTER™ *Series*

- *Advanced Turkey Hunting*
- *Advanced Whitetail Hunting*
- *America's Favorite Wild Game Recipes*
- *Bowhunting Equipment & Skills*
- *The Complete Guide to Hunting*
- *Cooking Wild in Kate's Kitchen*
- *Cooking Wild in Kate's Camp*
- *Dog Training*
- *Dressing & Cooking Wild Game*
- *Duck Hunting*
- *Elk Hunting*
- *Game Bird Cookery*
- *Hunting Record-Book Bucks*
- *Mule Deer Hunting*
- *Muzzleloading*
- *Pronghorn Hunting*
- *Venison Cookery*
- *Whitetail Techniques & Tactics*
- *Wild Turkey*

The Freshwater Angler™ *Series*

- *Advanced Bass Fishing*
- *All-Time Favorite Fish Recipes*
- *The Art of Fly Tying*
- *The Art of Fly Tying – CD ROM*
- *The Art of Freshwater Fishing*
- *The Complete Guide to Freshwater Fishing*
- *Fishing for Catfish*
- *Fishing Rivers & Streams*
- *Fishing Tips & Tricks*
- *Fishing With Artificial Lures*
- *Fly Fishing for Trout in Streams*
- *Fly Fishing for Beginners*
- *Largemouth Bass*
- *Modern Methods of Ice Fishing*
- *The New Cleaning & Cooking Fish*
- *Northern Pike & Muskie*
- *Panfish*
- *Smallmouth Bass*
- *Successful Walleye Fishing*
- *Trout*

The Complete FLY FISHERMAN™ *Series*

- *Fishing Dry Flies – Surface Presentations for Trout in Streams*
- *Fishing Nymphs, Wet Flies & Streamers – Subsurface Techniques for Trout in Streams*
- *Fly-Fishing Equipment & Skills*
- *Fly-Tying Techniques & Patterns*

To purchase these or other titles, contact your local bookseller, or visit our web site at www.creativepub.com.